Palestine and the Gulf States

Middle East Studies
History, Politics, and Law

SHAHROUGH AKHAVI, *General Editor*

Turkey in Germany
The Transnational Sphere of Deutschkei
Betigül Ercan Argun

Islamic Law, Epistemology and Modernity
Legal Philosophy in Contemporary Iran
Ashk P. Dahlén

Gender, Literacy, and Empowerment in Morocco
Fatima Agnaou

Trapped Between the Map and Reality
Geography and Perceptions of Kurdistan
Maria T. O'Shea

Kurdish Nationalism and Political Islam in Turkey
Kemalist Identity in Transition
Omer Taspinar

Organizations, Gender, and the Culture of Palestinian Activism in Haifa, Israel
Elizabeth Faier

Palestinian Identity in Jordan and Israel
The Necessary 'Other' in the Making of a Nation
Riad M. Nasser

Strategies of Resistance in the Dramatic Texts of North African Women
A Body of Words
Laura Chakravarty Box

Islam, Democracy, and the Status of Women
The Case of Kuwait
Helen Mary Rizzo

Legislating Authority
Sin and Crime in the Ottoman Empire and Turkey
Ruth A. Miller

War and Migration
Social Networks and Economic Strategies of the Hazaras of Afghanistan
Alessandro Monsutti

Sharaf Politics
Honor and Peacemaking in Israeli-Palestinian Society
Sharon D. Lang

The Accidental Tourist, Wilfrid Scawen Blunt, and the British Invasion of Egypt in 1882
Michael D. Berdine

Diplomacy and Displacement
Reconsidering the Turco-Greek Exchange of Populations, 1922–1934
Onur Yıldırım

Palestine and the Gulf States
The Presence at the Table
Rosemarie Said Zahlan

Palestine and the Gulf States

The Presence at the Table

Rosemarie Said Zahlan

Routledge
Taylor & Francis Group
New York   London

First published 2009
by Routledge
270 Madison Ave, New York, NY 10016

Simultaneously published in the UK
by Routledge
2 Park Square, Milton Park, Abingdon, Oxon OX14 4RN

Routledge is an imprint of the Taylor & Francis Group, an informa business

© 2009 Rosemarie Said Zahlan

Typeset in Sabon by IBT Global.
Printed and bound in the United States of America on acid-free paper by IBT Global.

All rights reserved. No part of this book may be reprinted or reproduced or utilised in any form or by any electronic, mechanical, or other means, now known or hereafter invented, including photocopying and recording, or in any information storage or retrieval system, without permission in writing from the publishers.

Trademark Notice: Product or corporate names may be trademarks or registered trademarks, and are used only for identification and explanation without intent to infringe.

Library of Congress Cataloging in Publication Data
Zahlan, Rosemarie Said.
 Palestine and the Gulf States : the presence at the table / by Rosemarie Said Zahlan.
  p. cm.—(Middle East studies : history, politics, and law)
 Includes bibliographical references and index.
 1. Persian Gulf Region—Foreign relations—Palestine. 2. Palestine—Foreign relations—Persian Gulf Region. 3. Palestine—Politics and government—1948–
 4. Palestine—Politics and government—1917–1948. I. Title.
 DS326.Z36 2009
 956.04—dc22
 2009005234

ISBN10: 0-415-80496-5 (hbk)
ISBN10: 0-203-87293-2 (ebk)

ISBN13: 978-0-415-80496-7 (hbk)
ISBN13: 978-0-203-87293-2 (ebk)

Table of Contents

List of Abbreviations   vii
Acknowledgments   ix

1   Introduction   1

2   Palestine and the Gulf States   15

3   Iran and Suez, 1953–1956   27

4   Impact of the 1967 War   36

5   The 1973 Arab-Israeli War and the Oil Boycott   47

6   The 1980s: Decade of Change   65

7   The United Nations: The Triangle without Corners   81

8   The 1990s   91

Notes   101
Bibliography   111
Index   113

Abbreviations

AIPAC	American Israel Public Affairs Committee
BAPCO	Bahrain Petroleum Company
DOP	Declaration of Principles
EC	European Community
GCC	Gulf Cooperation Council
OAPEC	Organisation of Arab Petroleum-Exporting Countries
OIC	Organisation of the Islamic Conference
OIR	Office of Intelligence Research
OPEC	Organisation of Petroleum-Exporting Countries
PFLP	Popular Front for the Liberation of Palestine
PLO	Palestine Liberation Organisation
UAE	United Arab Emirates
UNRWA	United Nations Relief and Works Agency

Acknowledgments

My wife, Rosemarie Said Zahlan, completed this work before she died on 10 May 2006, unexpectedly from the devastation that chemotherapy inflicts on the immune system. She did everything in her power to prepare her manuscript but alas she was unable to make it ready for publication. This task was left for me.

Rosemarie had a prodigious memory and could remember information for years. She thus did not commit to paper until she was ready to go to the printer. As a result her notes concerning acknowledgements were incomplete. Though we discussed at length our respective work I was not familiar with all her professional contacts and friends. So I apologise to those who may have discussed this subject with her but are not properly acknowledged and thanked.

Thanks are due to: Mr. Jasim Alsaggar who provided the detailed information on his sister, Shaha Hamad Alsaggar and her support for the 1936 Palestine uprising; Sally Morphet for valuable information on the Palestine Problem in the UN; Ambassador Hermann F. Ellis for first hand information on events during his ambassadorship in Saudi Arabia; John E. Peterson for information and for many valuable discussions of Gulf history.

During the process of preparing the manuscript for publication I benefited from scholarly advice by Ussama Makdisi, Souad Dajani, Yezid Sayegh, Naseeer Aruri, Nadia Hijab, and Mona Nsouli.

I am also indebted to Soraya Al-Turki, Shelagh Weir and Shahrough Akhavi for guidance in matters of editing and publication. I thank Marigold Acland for directing me to Mary Starkey whose efficient editorial work helped immeasurably.

I would like to thank Shahrough Akhavi, Gary Sick; Jean, Halla and Karim Makdisi and Benjamin Holtzman for their contributions to the selection of the title of the book.

Unpublished Crown Copyright material in the India Office Library and Records and in the Public Record Office transcribed here appears by permission of the Controller of Her Majesty's Stationery Office.

Antoine Zahlan
Beirut, January 2009

1 Introduction

The Arab world has been dominated by the question of Palestine since the early years of the twentieth century. Practically all political events of any significance have been related in one way or another to what is variously known as the Arab–Israeli dispute, the Middle East crisis, the Palestine–Israel problem and other appellations. During the first half of the century, the repercussions of the issue were confined largely to the greater Middle East and, to a much lesser extent, to Muslim India.

After the Second World War, however, the Palestine Question gradually shifted to occupy centre stage in international affairs. The creation of Israel in 1948, followed by the enforced exodus of Palestinians from their homes, resulted in what became known as 'the refugee problem'. It also directly and indirectly resulted in cataclysmic internal upheavals in neighbouring Arab states, which were beginning to assume their independence from the crumbling British and French empires.

The 1952 revolution in Egypt is one case of note. It occurred in partial response to the 1948 Arab military defeats. Gamal Abdel Nasser and his fellow conspirators had fought together in the Egyptian army against the invading Zionists who sought to establish a state in Palestine. The frustration of the young Egyptian officers at the inherent weaknesses of their army and leadership drew them together. It was inevitable perhaps that they would focus on the many flaws and failings of their own government. This was the genesis of the movement leading to the July 1952 revolution, which overthrew the monarchy and established a socialist republic in its place.

Mohamed Heikal, a journalist and close confidant of Nasser, has estimated that no less than 112 revolutions, coups or attempted coups took place in the Arab world in the first twenty-three years after the creation of Israel—that is between 1948 and 1971.[1] There have of course been many more since. With one military defeat after another, anger and frustration have inevitably led to further turmoil throughout the Arab world. The persistent US support of Israel in the face of international condemnation has deepened the anger and slowed down movement towards a civil society. Instead of embarking on modernisation after the end of colonialism, the Arab states have been severely restricted by military–political realities.

2 Palestine and the Gulf States

Reform has been stymied. This is not due to any shortage of human and financial resources; on the contrary, both are in place and can be compared favourably with those of many other developing and developed states.

Arab militarisation as a result of overpowering Israeli victories over the years has led to the polarisation of national resources, both human and financial, in the face what they have invariably regarded as a colonial settler state in their midst. This militarisation has grown after every Arab–Israeli war. Marked by military defeat, those states that are most vulnerable to attack have engaged in a futile arms race. During the Cold War, moreover, this carried the added dimension of political partisanship. This meant further complications in the international arena, and much greater costs in time, effort and expenditure. It is practically impossible to gauge the full extent of Arab military spending since 1948, but there is no question that it has been enormous.

In September 1964, President Lyndon Johnson sent John McCloy to Egypt to persuade Nasser to limit his purchase of missiles. Nasser told the US envoy that the problem in the Middle East had nothing to do with missiles: it was Palestine. Nothing could stop the arms race except a solution to the problem of Palestine and all that entailed.[2] This is a theme that was to be repeated in different forms and variations, and that continues until the present day: the problem of Palestine remains at the root of Arab affairs and, by extension, of international affairs.

On the international level, there have been many attempts to solve and/or defuse the dispute. There have been peace plans, attempts to put together peace plans, attempts to organise peace talks, peace initiatives, etc. These have included the Rogers Plan, the Schultz peace initiative, the Nixon Plan, the Fahd Plan, the Venice Declaration, the Peace Process, the Road Map and many others. There have been bilateral talks, trilateral talks, multilateral talks—all to no avail.

A recent study by Bercovitch and Regan analysed the number and nature of 'protracted conflicts' around the world which they defined as enduring conflicts. The Arab–Israeli conflict was of course regarded as one of these. The authors calculated that there were no less than seventy-five conflict-management efforts between Egypt and Israel alone for the period 1948–79; twenty-four between Jordan and Israel for 1948–86; and thirty-eight between Syria and Israel for 1948–92.[3] There have been many more since, particularly between Israel and the Palestinians, the Palestine Liberation Organisation (PLO), the Palestinian National Authority and the Palestine Authority.

The question of Palestine continues to dominate international affairs into the twenty-first century. In March 2003, on the eve of the US invasion of Iraq, President George W. Bush announced his plan to unveil the Road Map to Middle East peace. His secretary of state, Colin Powell, had led up to this announcement a few days earlier by underlining the president's personal commitment to this policy. This cynical revival of yet another

Arab–Israeli peace plan at such a critical point in time was not lost on many. It was a not-too-subtle acknowledgement, made perhaps for the first time, of the strong links between events in Palestine and the Gulf.

By the end of 2005 the Road Map had been phased out of US policy, to be replaced by a new policy which almost totally disregards the Arab–Israeli conflict.

PALESTINE AND THE GULF

The Palestine question provides a useful starting point for this study, for it is indelibly intertwined with the US invasion of Iraq, particularly the run-up to hostilities. International outrage, expressed in massive anti-war demonstrations worldwide, decried the double standards of US foreign policy which ignored Israeli violations of UN resolutions, all the while relying on dubious evidence to try and prove Iraqi violations and thereby create a *casus belli*. Bush's famous line that 'this war is all about peace' was an apt reference to the relationship.

This book is about the relationships between Palestine and the Gulf which have existed since the 1930s. They have ebbed and flowed, they have started and they have declined, they have criss-crossed barriers and events, and they have taken on different forms. There have been connections and there have been mutual influences. They have pervaded national, regional and international relationships. They have been bilateral and they have been multi-lateral. They have occurred in different guises and they have appeared and disappeared unexpectedly from the public arena.

Surprisingly, this network of links and relationships has remained largely unknown, for a variety of reasons which will be discussed in this book. It was rarely alluded to until just a few years ago. In 1999, it was rather tentatively brought up by Gary Sick of Columbia University as 'the ghost at the table'[4] in an article in which he disclosed an 'intriguing record' of mutual influence between the two. Although the article was about the 1980s and 1990s, the relationship actually started in the 1930s. This was recognised by British statesmen well before the Second World War. When he was British secretary of foreign affairs in 1942, Anthony Eden famously admitted to his staff that Britain would never be able to formulate an identifiable and suitable Middle East policy so long as the problem of Palestine remained unsolved.

This book sets out to show that the presence at the table is not that of a ghostly figure; it is substantial, dominant and omnipresent. But it has long been ignored and/or denied.

In the early years, the linkage was recognised and acted on—first by Britain and then by the US government at the highest level. President Roosevelt promised King Abdel Aziz that the USA would make no decision on Palestine without full consultation with Arabs and Jews alike. He also assured the king in his capacity as chief of the executive branch of the US government that he would take no action that might prove hostile to the Arab people.[5] As late as 1957, in an effort to enlist the support of Saudi Arabia for his doctrine in the Middle East, President Eisenhower assured Crown Prince (later King) Faisal that the USA would always oppose any expansion by Israel at the expense of its neighbours.[6]

Two well-known links between Palestine and the Gulf require little introduction. The first was established in 1948 by the arrival in the Gulf states of homeless Palestinians seeking jobs in public and private institutions; such institutions had been created since the late 1940s with the vast economic expansion that accompanied the discovery of oil. The different waves of Palestinians arriving in the Gulf generally corresponded with the successive crises they faced at home. Each upheaval created another wave of migration: first 1948, then 1967, then 1970, 1973 and 1976. With time, Palestinians established communities which grew in size and influence. Their presence constitutes a visible and dynamic link between Palestine and the Gulf.

The second link has been forged by the large financial donations made by the rulers, governments and citizens of the Gulf states to the social and economic welfare of Palestinians, whether at home or abroad. These donations began in the 1930s when the states were poor, and have grown through the years, as they have become increasingly wealthy. It is almost impossible to provide an accurate estimate of the extent of this financial support. But there is no doubt that it has been enormous, and has provided the main sustenance for a large proportion of Palestinian individuals, families, institutions and organisations at home and in the Diaspora.

There have been (and will continue to be) many other links and relationships between Palestine and the Gulf. This book seeks to discuss the most outstanding. It will analyse the strength of the relationships between them throughout the twentieth century and explore those that have remained largely unrecognised. Such relations include and transcend individuals; they extend to the organisational, socio-cultural, economic and political levels.

Networks and Linkages

The relationships between Palestine and Palestinians, on the one hand, and the people and governments of the Gulf States and Saudi Arabia, on the other, can be likened to networks with two focal points. The formation of this field of linkages emerges from the commonality of language, religion, culture, history and from the place of Jerusalem in Islam.

The relationships between the two populations are reciprocal, yet they are not symmetrical. This is natural, responding as it does to the needs and conditions of both sides of the relationship. Both parties have influenced each other in different ways. These differences constitute the asymmetry in the linkages.

A third factor has been superimposed onto this field of linkages. It is far more powerful than the other two, and differs from them both qualitatively and quantitatively. It activates the field and at the same time provides much of its dynamism, negative and positive. This is the role of the hegemonic superpower: Britain until 1948, and the USA thereafter.

Since the early twentieth century, and largely after the end of the First World War, there has been a long sequence of triangular interaction between the three which with time became a constant factor in Arab politics. This factor has also varied in time and place, but nevertheless has been present at most critical junctures of Arab and international politics.

In this triangular relationship, the influence of the superpower cannot be reciprocated by the other two. Its impact on the Palestine problem is overwhelming, yet the Palestinians can only bring an infinitesimal influence to bear on it. The Gulf states, by contrast, have greater leverage by dint of their vast oil reserves, their enormous financial assets and their vital geostrategic location. At specific points in time, they have applied this leverage to promote a willingness, if nothing else, to tackle the problem. But the asymmetrical relationship between the three components of the triangle can be said to have resulted in paralysis; this has impeded significant progress in resolving a crisis that has become one of the most omnipresent and intractable in the world.

The operational aspects of this linkage are an important focus of this book. It will be shown that what happens in Palestine affects the Gulf states internally. It plays a role in the dynamics of their political apparatus. It then causes them to play a different role on the international stage.

Formation of the Field of Linkages

The exact moment of the creation of the field is difficult to pinpoint. Its genesis can doubtless be found in the 1917 Balfour Declaration, which contained the seeds of the conflict that was to form and shape the Palestine problem.

The field itself was first manifested during the 1930s when a variety of events concurred. These included the establishment of the kingdom of Saudi Arabia in 1932; the opening up of the Gulf region to oil companies in search of petroleum deposits and concessions; and the establishment of a British air route to India with landing and fuelling stations on the Arab coast of the Gulf.

These created a new dynamism in the Gulf region, which was enhanced by the establishment of improved communications of all kinds. Most outstanding was the introduction of the radio: it had a remarkable impact on people who were still lacking in education and who were isolated from the rest of the world by the immense power of British policies, as well as by geographical remoteness, poverty and the absence of all modern forms of communication. In 1936, radio broadcasts in Arabic began to be beamed to the coast of Arabia from Bari (Italy), followed shortly by Iraqi, German and

British radio stations. A network of roads was constructed, linking the region with hitherto inaccessible locations and gradually lifting its long isolation.

At around the same time, Britain established refuelling and landing stations on the Arab coasts of the Gulf for its civil and military aircraft. The arrival and departure of passengers, albeit only in transit, created another avenue of communications with the rest of the world. The new role of some Gulf ports as entrepôts was enhanced after the discovery of oil in Bahrain in 1931. The influx of foreign oil-company workers and executives contributed to an awareness of events beyond the shores of the Gulf.

In 1936, the Palestinians called a general strike to protest against rising Jewish immigration from Nazi Europe. They wanted the British mandatory government to stop sanctioning the arrival of the refugees, who were fast becoming a destabilising force in the country. The claims of these immigrants to Palestine naturally aroused fear among the Palestinians that they would ultimately be displaced by the foreigners. The general strike caused great hardship throughout the country as economic life ground to a halt. The introduction of British emergency regulations inevitably led to conflict.

News of events in Palestine reached the Gulf. There was for the first time an awareness of the many dangers facing the Palestinians. The Peel Commission report, published in 1937, recommended partition of the country. This recommendation shocked the Arab world and aroused great sympathy for the Palestinians, who now faced the possibility of losing half their country.

The response of the people and governments of the Gulf states and Saudi Arabia to the 1936–9 strike and the rebellion that followed marked the beginning of the relationship between these two sides of the triangle. These early beginnings have remained largely unknown for a variety of reasons. They will be reconstructed in this book from declassified US and British government archives as well as from publications, and from private interviews with protagonists and/or their descendants.

The most memorable example of linkage was the oil embargo following the October 1973 Arab–Israeli war. Led by Saudi Arabia, Algeria and the small Gulf states, it linked the withholding of oil sales with the withdrawal of Israeli forces from Gaza and the West Bank. Arab oil-producing states were exasperated with US policy, and were particularly incensed when, in July 1973, the USA used its veto for the fifth time in UN history to block a Security Council resolution deploring the continuing Israeli occupation.

The linkage was acknowledged worldwide as the boycott began to bite, causing inflation and recession. Western concessions to the Palestinians followed. The question of Palestine emerged the next year as an independent agenda item at the United Nations; for the first time the self-determination and human rights of the Palestinians, not only their status as refugees, were acknowledged. And the PLO gradually transmorphed from isolation to international recognition and diplomatic status.

In 1998, when the USA was preparing to launch a vast aerial bombardment of Iraq ('Desert Fox'), anti-war demonstrations spread throughout many countries in the Arab world and the West. One of the most memorable protests occurred at Ohio State University when Secretary of State Madeleine Albright, National Security Adviser Sandy Berger and Secretary of Defence William Cohen appeared on live TV in an effort to explain and promote government policy. They were clearly unprepared for the response awaiting them. They were visibly shaken by the heckling of the academic audience, which was angered by their own government's double standards in militarily enforcing UN resolutions for Iraq, all the while condoning Israel's flouting of many more such resolutions.

This Gulf–Palestine linkage during the months preceding Desert Fox was driven home on the military level. Saudi Arabia, Bahrain and other Gulf states refused access to US forces in the face of the continued deterioration of the situation in Palestine. High-level visits by US officials to persuade these countries to provide access proved unsuccessful. It was not coincidental, therefore, that President Clinton visited Gaza in December 1998. There he addressed the Palestine National Council, opened the newly built airport and visited the town. It was the first ever visit of a US president, and as such earned wide media coverage.

With that out of the way, Clinton could then proceed to the business at hand: bombing Iraq. The day after he returned home, he ordered the bombing raid on Iraq. Gulf rulers could no longer object.

The role of right-wing think tanks and neo-cons in White House policy making since 11 September 2001 is well known. I have singled out a 1995 article by one of them, Zalmay Khalilzad, a former US ambassador to Iraq: 'The United States and the Persian Gulf: preventing regional hegemony'.[7] It emphasises the vital strategic importance of the Gulf to the USA, and promotes a policy to preclude the dominance of either Iraq or Iran, at the same time encouraging a balance of power between the two. It advocates strengthening US military ties with the Gulf Cooperation Council (GCC) states, and proposes a long-term role for Israel as a partner with the GCC states in promoting Gulf security.

The perspective of Gulf–Palestine linkage inherent in this and similar publications and statements is predicated on the assumption that the Gulf states are not an integral part of the Arab world, and that their relationships with other Arab countries can be altered at will, shuffled and manipulated.

Neither the Gulf nor the problem of Palestine is contained by geographical boundaries, especially in the computer–satellite age. Palestine continues to evoke powerful sentiments. Satellite imagery has brought home the impact of the intifada and the dramatic realities of daily life under occupation; combined with the instant access to information provided by the internet, these pictures have deepened rather than diminished national, religious, cultural and social ties.

By disregarding this linkage, or denying its centrality, the USA has moved from one serious crisis to another. Anthony Eden's admission about Middle Eastern policy has yet to resonate in the State Department.

Persistent policy decisions which view the Arab–Israeli situation as distinct and different from the Gulf expose the region to great danger and will invariably collapse.

TWIN PILLARS: SAUDI ARABIA AND ISRAEL

The buzz words of 'dual containment' towards Iraq and Iran throughout most of the 1990s could well have been applied to another aspect of US foreign relations. Likewise, an earlier term, 'twin pillar', the US policy in the Gulf during the 1970s—the pillars being Saudi Arabia and Iran—is more suitably applied to another doctrine, one that has been far more durable.

Ironically, both terms ('dual containment' and 'twin pillar') describe more accurately the most constant aspects of US policy towards the Near/Middle East since the Second World War. These are the twin-track relationships with Saudi Arabia and Israel. A brief survey of US policy in the Middle East and North Africa during the past six decades reveals immense fluctuations in US bilateral relations with the states and governments of the region; by contrast, its dealings with Israel and Saudi Arabia have been characterised by great consistency.

US–Egyptian relations since 1945, for example, fluctuated from the tentative warmth during the early years of the Free Officers to the anger and bitterness following the 1967 Arab–Israeli war, to the heady efforts of the Sadat years, and the sobering moments of the 1990s. US–Iraqi, US–Tunisian, US–Syrian, US–Libyan and other relationships have likewise varied enormously with the years and with the issues involved.

But the 'twin pillars' of US policy, Saudi Arabia and Israel, have been constant throughout the post-war period. The US–Saudi relationship was born after US oil companies first entered Saudi Arabia, and was given added depth by the personal friendship forged between King Abdel Aziz and President Roosevelt. This relationship has been one of the most constant aspects of US foreign policy in general, not only in the Middle East. It was acknowledged and strengthened after the 1957 visit to the USA of King Saud, and has steadily grown in substance, particularly after the 1967 Arab–Israeli war ushered in a period of decline for Egypt and Syria.

The US–Israeli relationship, tentative in the beginning, has also developed substantially since the 1960s. By the early twenty-first century it has become of paramount importance to both. Its security has become intertwined with that of the USA and it has evolved to become a vital element in US domestic politics. This has been recognised in elections, whether of governors, senators or congressional representatives; and more recently it has assumed an essential role in the selection and administration of academic funding.[8]

The twin relationships with Saudi Arabia and Israel have dominated US post-war policy in the Middle East. The first has been based, very generally speaking, on economic considerations, the second on security. They have existed alongside one another for over fifty years. They have remained in parallel; the few times they have become conjoined were linked mostly with the conflict in Palestine. One example occurred in 1969–70, and was encapsulated in an intriguing episode recounted by John D. Rockefeller in his autobiography.

After the June 1967 war, and the rapid decline in US–Arab relations as a result of US support for Israel, Rockefeller, in his capacity as chairman of Chase Bank, wanted to spearhead the revival of these relations. He was encouraged by Eugene Black, former head of the World Bank and financial adviser to the Emir of Kuwait.

In late 1969, Rockefeller was approached by the Egyptian ambassador to the UN with an invitation to meet President Nasser, who was interested in re-establishing meaningful contacts with the USA. Rockefeller saw this as a potentially significant opening, but wanted his government's approval before embarking on anything new. So he flew to Washington to see the national security adviser, Henry Kissinger, who had previously worked as an aide to Nelson Rockefeller. Kissinger encouraged him in the venture, and asked him to brief President Nixon after his return from Egypt.

Nasser welcomed Rockefeller warmly. His message was straightforward. He undertook to obtain recognition of Israel's right to exist from all Arab countries if Israel implemented UN Resolution 242. Nasser said that the resolution, which called for Israeli withdrawal from land occupied in the 1967 war, would provide the general framework for a peace agreement. He also undertook to support minor border rectifications and the demilitarisation of the Golan Heights once the UN resolution was implemented.

Rockefeller then went on to Saudi Arabia where he met King Faisal. The king had inflexible opinions regarding US policy in the Arab world, and also wanted implementation of the UN resolution. This encouraged Rockefeller to press for a change in US policy when he returned home, with the Egyptian offer as a useful starting point.

He mentioned his observations to Kissinger, and a month later was invited to the White House for what he assumed would be a private meeting with Nixon and Kissinger. He was taken aback to discover the meeting was not private at all: senior oil executives, including the chairmen of Standard Oil, Mobil and Amoco, were present, together with others. It was inevitable, perhaps, that details of the meeting were then leaked to the press. Some newspapers shrilly decried the sinister role of oil and banking interests and saw them as instrumental in promoting a change in US policy to Israel.

The outrage in the press, radio and TV took Rockefeller totally by surprise. Long-established accounts at Chase were cancelled—anathema to any bank—and he was harangued in the press. He was attacked personally. *Newsweek*, for example, entitled its article about the incident 'Rockefeller: blinded by oil?'[9] This violent reaction to his well-meaning attempt to promote a new departure led him to surmise that he had been deliberately set up precisely to prevent any changes in US policy. He backed down and never brought the subject up again. The twin-pillar policy had reverted to parallel lines.

UNDISCOVERED GULF

Serious literature on the Gulf is sparse because there has been a paucity of scholars devoted to studying the region in depth and over time. One consequence is that the relationship between the Gulf and the Palestine problem has been ignored or downplayed. These restrictions are due to a number of factors, some closely allied with the enormous wealth the region has enjoyed for the past three or four decades.

Another reason for the paucity of serious scholarly studies on the Gulf is the common assumption there is little in the region worthy of research—an attitude which has been reinforced by the sycophantic literature. As a result most observers, even those acquainted with the region, assume that it is the recent wealth of the Gulf states which has inspired the available literature, and that there is little else worthy of scholarly consideration.

In the late 1970s, for example, the British director of an Anglo-Arab trade organisation—a former British diplomat with a lifetime of experience in the Arab world—described the internal history of the United Arab Emirates, as being 'at least until the discovery of oil frankly too trivial to contribute much of value to the *study of mankind*".[10] He thus dismissed the history of the UAE as beyond even anthropological interest. Such an attitude denigrates the society and weakens the possibility of serious research.

Because Gulf scholars as a community are still weak and disorganised, they have tolerated persons in their midst who are not professionally qualified. The outcome has resulted in an undermining of the quality of their discipline.

The universities of the Gulf states, of course, should be in the vanguard of innovative research on their region. And a number of excellent scholars from different Gulf states, who obtained their Ph.D.s in the West, have returned home, some to teach, some to work in government or in private institutions and research centres. The scholarly output from and on the region is growing, but it remains limited. The support system for research is still in an embryonic phase. And quality is not perceived widely enough as a priority. It is all too often overtaken by the need to avoid contentious issues. 'Happy history' is often regarded as more important than the truth. And publishers do not enforce high standards of research and editing.

One might expect that publications emanating from the region would set the pace for the field. But the weaknesses of local output have enabled foreign concerns, such as the security of oil supplies or the economics of immigrant labour, to dominate the literature.

The Gulf states are overwhelmingly viewed as a source for capital and employment, and a vast international market for weapons and consumer goods. A disproportionate amount is written on labour movements, for example, and the military, often without due awareness of the interests of the home population. This type of literature reflects largely non-Gulf interests, not local interests and concerns. Such literature cannot therefore be classified as Gulf Studies.

Another category of work could be loosely referred to as 'safe literature': books and articles about the environment, exotic animals, dhows, falconry, pearls, camels, Bedouins, etc. While some of these do make significant contributions, the remainder by and large tend to be limited in scope and add little to an understanding of the subject.

Maybe the most striking feature, particularly as seen in the subject matter of this book, has been the marginalisation of the role of the Gulf states in modern Arab affairs. Most studies on the modern Arab world, and indeed most students of the modern Arab world, focus their attention on Egypt and the Fertile Crescent first and foremost, and then the Maghreb. That is where the epicentre of the region is considered to be.

This appears to be the continuation of a long tradition which was introduced and maintained by the British government of India: it emanated from a policy of isolating the small Gulf states from the rest of the world. Since Britain controlled the entry and exit of people from these states, it was relatively easy to pursue such a policy; the poverty of the states during the pre-oil era inadvertently strengthened it. One British official admitted in the 1930s that Britain guarded the Gulf states in the manner of a jealous husband.

INSTANT EXPERTS

Since 1990, when Iraq invaded Kuwait and catapulted the Gulf into the international arena, a new problem regarding an understanding of the region was created. This was the rise of 'instant experts': writers, commentators, analysts, broadcasters and others who professed a knowledge of the Gulf. They have demonstrated a breathtaking ability to superimpose their own fields of interest onto Gulf affairs. It seems in many cases as if political theories have been transplanted from textbooks.

These experts contributed significantly to an international awareness of the region. Millions of people worldwide became familiar with previously unknown words such as 'Kuwait', 'bidoons', 'amir', 'Qatar', 'Bahrain', etc. Maps of the region were shown on TV and published in newspapers in order to place the Gulf in some sort of geographical perspective.

Only a few of these experts had either been trained in Middle Eastern/ Arab/Islamic history, politics, economics or sociology or had had serious professional contact with the Gulf. Their knowledge of the Gulf was very limited indeed; many seemed to assume that it was an extension of Egypt, Syria, Jordan or Lebanon. They plunged headlong into analyses of places and societies with which they were strikingly unfamiliar. The literature and body of knowledge was sparse, so they filled the gaps ad hoc with minimal preparation and well-worn clichés about Arabs and Islam.

Regardless of social and political nuance, they forged ahead with their own theories—and one of the most important was their own take on the Palestine problem. In their haste to appear familiar with the territory they were covering, they fell in with hearsay and continued the old adage that there were no links between Palestine and the Gulf.

A major characteristic of Gulf linkages with Palestine—and one which has not been recognised sufficiently—has been their perception in the West. It will be seen how, during the height of its numerous crises over the general strike of 1936–9 throughout Palestine, the British government regarded the king of Saudi Arabia both as the key to the solution of the problem and as the most compelling reason to find a solution. This focus on Saudi Arabia as the fulcrum for the resolution of the crisis occurred long before the petroleum potential of the country was known.

Determined British attempts to resolve the Palestine crisis during the late 1930s were in direct response to their perception of the role of Saudi Arabia as the pivotal power of the Arab world. The inconsistencies of the Balfour Declaration and the strategically fraught problems of steadily expanding Jewish immigration to Palestine commanded a surprisingly inferior position in the policy-making institutions of the British government.

Another aspect of the linkages, once again not widely known, manifested itself in the impact of the Palestine problem on local affairs. It will be shown how anti-British feelings in Kuwait were exacerbated by the 1936–9 strike in Palestine; these feelings polarised the opposition, ultimately leading to the establishment of the *majlis* movement there in 1938. In other parts of the Gulf region, it led to different kinds of expressions of Arab and Islamic feelings. These were to grow rather than abate with time, much as the Palestine crisis has grown and its repercussions diffused over the past century.

The nexus between Palestine and the Gulf includes personal interactions. Some notable examples are

- that Fatah was founded in Kuwait, where Yasser Arafat and his colleagues were living and working in the 1950s;
- that the brother of the amir of Kuwait, Shaikh Fahd bin Ahmad, was a member of Fatah, first when it was based in Jordan and then later after it moved to Lebanon; he was arrested in 1971 as a fighter in Lebanon and repatriated to Kuwait;[11]
- that many Palestinians earned fortunes in the Gulf, mostly as contractors but also as advisers and bankers, and later made generous financial donations to members of their extended families, to their

home towns and to social, cultural and economic Palestinian institutions at home and abroad. A quick glance at the members of the Board of Trustees of the Welfare Association, the leading Palestinian welfare institution, will reveal the Gulf origins of their individual wealth; they are Palestinians who lived and worked in Gulf states such as Kuwait, the UAE, Qatar and Saudi Arabia. Their generous funding of Palestinian educational, social and economic projects can be seen as another facet of the networked field of relationships;[12]

- that countless other Palestinian organisations, based in the Arab world and abroad, have been sponsored by individuals who earned their wealth in the Gulf.

During the period leading up to and immediately after British withdrawal from the Gulf in 1971, a number of seminars, workshops, conferences, studies, etc were hurriedly organised by a variety of Western universities, think tanks, research centres and others. They were anxious to forecast the security of the region and particularly concerned about who or what would fill the 'vacuum' created by Britain's departure.

Many of these deliberations revealed the lack of knowledge of the participants, a constant theme in the modern literature of the Gulf. They considered, erroneously as it turned out, that the Palestinians of the Gulf would become the major destabilising force there. Once again, the Gulf 'experts' of that early period were transposing many of their own attitudes and perceptions. It is interesting to note in the statements and publications that followed those conferences that there was an almost total absence of foresight regarding the disruption that the Baathi regime of Iraq could inflict on individual states and the region as a whole. Within a decade, the short-sightedness of these 'experts' was revealed: Iraq invaded first Iran and then, a decade later, Kuwait, setting the area alight for many years to come. At the same time, the 'destabilisation' caused by Palestinian residents, the dreaded 'fifth column', proved to be yet another phantom.

Hopefully, this book will serve as a starting point for further studies. Only a brief attempt is made here to fully analyse the motivation of various Gulf rulers to sway and influence the superpower vis-à-vis the Palestine problem. Many theorists have claimed that these rulers acted either to deflect criticism from their people or to promote themselves as great leaders, or both. But little evidence to support such interpretations has ever been provided. Other studies could focus on the internal impact in the Gulf of events in Palestine and compare them with the impact in other Arab states. Comparative analyses on this subject are lacking in the literature of the modern Arab world.

Moreover, as illustrated by so many contemporary events, the USA has never been able to fully perceive the strength of the Saudi position vis-à-vis Palestine. We have already noted what Anthony Eden acknowledged in 1942 and what Nasser underlined again in 1964. Despite these and many more acknowledgements, US policy makers bafflingly continued to ignore the reality.

Anthony Cordesman, an author with wide knowledge and experience of US–Saudi relations stated when Reagan first assumed office in 1981: 'A new US administration once again had to learn that the Saudi concern with the Palestinian issue was not a *pro forma* gesture, but a major political commitment.'[13] Practically every new US administration started out with a cynical attitude, and had to learn once again that Saudi policy was in response to the forces of Arab nationalism.

Almost two decades later, Cordesman underlined the linkage once again. As holder of the Burke Chair in Strategy, he conducted the CSIS Gulf in Transition Project whereby he developed a series of reports recommending US policy towards the Gulf. He concluded that Gulf security was inextricably linked to peace in the Middle East. It was important to the stability of the Gulf and to the maintenance of the US position there. 'A strong, highly visible and continuing US effort to find a solution . . . is more than an Arab–Israeli issue. It is critical to the Gulf to find security and to reduce the threat of terrorism.'[14]

Cordesman considered that the Arab–Israeli conflict undermined the ties between the southern Gulf states and the West, and that US policy could not consider the Gulf alone. If the USA failed to achieve a full peace settlement, he advised, it must at least make a convincing case to the Arabs and Iran that it was making every effort to do so. 'This means a full Presidential commitment to US engagement towards both Israel and the Palestinian Authority.'[15]

The first of these reports was written in October 2000, immediately before the presidential elections and as a guide to US policy in Gulf regardless of the outcome. He argued then that the Arab–Israeli conflict affected not only 'the hearts and minds of the entire region', but it also undermined the ties between the moderate Gulf States and the West.

By the twenty-first century, then, the multi-layered linkages between the two regions, the Gulf and Palestine, were beginning to be raised in the public domain. They have yet to be fully researched and analysed. This book is a first step.

2 Palestine and the Gulf States

There were three kinds of links between Palestine and the Gulf States: first, unofficial relationships, such as those between the people of the Gulf and the Palestinians; second, official connections, particularly those enunciated by governments and rulers; and third, the links between the two that were implicitly (and explicitly) acknowledged by the British, US and other non-Arab governments.

It will be seen how these links were perceived and ultimately shaped the policies of the British and US governments. Until the 1950s, they were mediated by the British government; and since then by that of the USA.

Some of these links will be investigated and placed within the framework of three major landmarks in the modern history of Palestine: the 1939 White Paper; the 1974 international acceptance of the PLO as sole representative of the Palestinians; and the 1982 Venice Declaration by the European Community (EC), which marked its departure from US policy on Israel.

It will be seen how Gulf–Palestinian links have existed for more than half a century, and how they were dealt a massive blow with the 1990 Iraqi invasion of Kuwait, which severely affected the relationship. The dramatic uncoupling that ensued set the Palestine problem adrift. It has since sought an anchor in Egypt, from which it has not secured any notable advantages to date.

THE PALESTINE PROBLEM AND THE GULF, 1936–9

Personal Links

Before the 1930s, the Gulf states were cut off from the outside world: no one was allowed in without a British visa, which was virtually impossible to obtain. Very few people, with the exception of a handful of leading merchants, could afford to go abroad.

The most significant ties of the region were with India: most trade was with Bombay; Indian merchants lived and worked throughout the Gulf states; they enjoyed a special position as British subjects; the Indian rupee was the main currency; political agents and residents were drawn from the select Political Service of the British government of India; and the British Indian navy policed the waters of the Gulf.

There were no local newspapers, although a few publications from Egypt and Iraq filtered through on an irregular and haphazard basis. A radical transformation occurred after broadcasting began. The Italian station at Bari, established in 1934 to promote Italian influence in the Arab world, was the first Arabic service to beam its radio programmes to the Gulf.[1] The second Arabic station was that of Kasr el-Zuhur, set up by King Ghazi in his palace in Baghdad.

The impact of these transmissions on what was then a predominantly illiterate society was dramatic: the news broadcasts from Bari rapidly became focal points of social and political life. The well-to-do of Bahrain and Kuwait, where electricity supplies were available, bought their own radios; those who could not afford to congregated in the coffee shops, where loudspeakers were attached to radios. In places such as Abu Dhabi and the other Trucial states, where there were no electricity supplies, car batteries were utilised to provide power for the radios. The BBC was slow to respond: it did not begin its own relay in Arabic until early 1938; and the Arabic service of Radio Berlin went on air in April 1939.

As the people of the Gulf tuned in to news bulletins, their first tenuous communication links with the Arab world to the north were just beginning. This coincided with the first major expression of Palestinian nationalism after the massive Jewish emigration from the anti-Semitism of the Third Reich began to take place: in April 1936, Palestinian demonstrations in Jaffa paved the way for the uprising in Palestine as a protest against British acceptance of the escalating pace of Jewish immigration.

A few days later, the Mufti, Hajj Amin Husseini, declared a general strike throughout the country; its demands were the termination of Jewish immigration, a ban on the sale of Arab land to Jews and the establishment of a Palestinian national government. This large-scale protest against British policy caught the imagination of the Arab and Muslim worlds, which viewed with alarm the potential displacement of the population by European immigrants. A few days later, the Arab Higher Committee, with the Mufti as its head, was established; it assumed the institutional leadership of the uprising, which lasted until 1939.

As the strike caused economic activity to grind to a halt, appeals were made for financial aid to sustain the serious losses the people were suffering. The earliest links between the Gulf states and Palestine took place at this time. Palestinian authorities wrote to the ruler of Kuwait, Shaikh Ahmad al-Jabir, in June inviting financial support of the strike. Mindful of his treaty conditions which forbade any foreign communications or correspondence, he refused, and forbade any public contributions to the fund to be made in Kuwait. But many saw fit to openly defy his orders despite the prevailing poverty of the Kuwaiti people; they collected a total of 200 Iraqi dinars, which were sent to Palestine in July 1936.

British officials in the Gulf were uneasy about the continuation of the strike, the course of which was followed assiduously by Arabs and Muslims everywhere. They were especially worried about the decline in British prestige, the main bulwark of its power in the Gulf, and realised that the exercise of British authority was being eroded by widespread sympathy for the Palestinians. Some Kuwaitis, for example, had circulated an Iraqi report about a massive anti-British uprising in India in support of the Palestinians which had resulted in more than a thousand dead.[2]

In October 1936, a seven-man committee (from the leading Ghanim, Khudayr, Bahr, Humaydi, Qanai merchant families), which had been formed in Kuwait to assist the Palestinians, called for a public meeting. The objective was to draw attention to the strike and raise money to support it. The ruler, clearly unable to stop the proceedings, discreetly left town on a hunting trip.

At least 150 people attended, including most of the leading merchants and notables. The meeting was marked by strong statements of unity with the Palestinian people, whose plight moved many to tears. The first person to make a contribution was the daughter of a merchant, Hamad al-Saqr, who unhesitatingly donated her own property as a strong gesture of support to the Palestinians. All in all, 9,500 rupees (equivalent then to £730, a substantial amount of money, particularly for the impecunious Kuwaitis) were collected. Over and above this sum, 200 lottery tickets, issued through an Iraqi newspaper, were sold very quickly.

The crisis in Palestine affected the Kuwaitis in another way. It had a strong impact on internal affairs, inadvertently reviving old resentments. In getting together to openly defy the ruler, attend the meeting and make financial donations, some of the participants also began to express their dissatisfaction with other matters at home. As such, they formed the nucleus of a movement calling for internal reform. Two of their principal objectives were to have a more representative government and a greater say in decision making.

The political opposition was exacerbated by the great poverty that had set in during the early 1930s as a result of the depression in Europe and the USA. This depression had caused a downturn in the pearling market; this was made more acute by the introduction of Japanese cultured pearls, which brought about an almost total collapse of the economic mainstay of Kuwait. The ruler, by contrast, was relatively well off, and had for the first time become financially independent of his people when he started receiving annual retainer fees from the oil companies, which were still in the exploratory phase.

The financial independence of the ruler had disrupted the interdependence that had existed for centuries between him and his people and which had been based on mutual need. The polarisation of ruler and opposition finally led to the imposition in 1938 by the latter of a legislative council, a *majlis*, to introduce internal reforms under the leadership of the ruler's popular cousin, Abdallah al-Salim.[3]

The people of Bahrain were also very concerned about Palestine, although they do not appear to have collected funds at this point in the crisis. But they circulated publications which called on Muslims everywhere to save the Palestinians from the horrors of British rule, including murder, the destruction of villages, and intolerable harassment and interference. In Dubai, collections were made for Palestine, as they were in Sharjah, where the ruler, Shaikh Sultan bin Saqr, donated a generous amount of money.[4]

Links of Rulers: King Abdel Aziz of Saudi Arabia

In May 1936, a Royal Commission presided over by Lord Peel was appointed in London to examine the situation and recommend a solution to the violence in Palestine. In November, a halt was called to the strike, and Palestinians returned to work, hoping for positive results from the Peel Commission.

When, in early July 1937, the Commission published its report recommending partition, a spontaneous and emotional response was registered throughout the Arab world. The possibility that a large part of Palestine would be given away to European Jewish immigrants, who had grown in number by 63 per cent since 1933 and who were still arriving, became real for the first time. The Palestinians were, of course, devastated; their fears were shared by their fellow Arabs.

Solidarity with Palestine was expressed throughout the Arab world. Arab nationalism and a call for unity in the face of imperial adversity were reflected in the press. Baghdad newspapers reported assiduously on the many stages of the unfolding tragedy. Baghdad radio, from the Kasr al-Zuhur palace of King Ghazi, carried the same message and was heard throughout the Gulf.

As Arab leaders gathered in Bludan outside Damascus in early September to discuss their response, no Gulf rulers joined them. They were excluded by dint of their treaty relations, which forbade any dealings with countries other than Britain. The ruler of Kuwait was reported to have asked the president of the conference, Naji al-Suwaidi (a former foreign minister of Iraq), to represent him, and sent telegrams to the kings of Saudi Arabia and Iraq and the colonial secretary to declare his support.[5]

In doing so, he risked British censure, since he had solemnly undertaken not to communicate with any foreign powers. Reactions to Palestine in the Gulf states were thereby strictly contained; the rulers and the people were allowed little access to the meetings and conferences taking place during the 1936–9 period.

This was not the case with Saudi Arabia, which was an independent and sovereign state. There the sentiments of the king were heard so frequently by British officials that they became increasingly alarmed at their own government's policies. Abdel Aziz rarely minced words or feelings when it came to Palestine; he made his reactions known to all who visited him.

George Rendel, principal at the Foreign Office, went to Saudi Arabia in 1937. The king spent many hours explaining to him the importance of an equitable solution to the problem. On his return home, Rendel aptly conveyed the gist of the king's arguments to his department: 'The Arab quarrel is not against the Jews in Palestine, nor . . . against the British. It is against the alien invaders who make no secret about wanting to transform Palestine from an Arab country into a Jewish country.'[6]

British policy on Palestine had reached an impasse. Obligations contained in the Balfour Declaration and other statements regarding a Jewish home were at odds with the realities on the ground. The strong Arab opposition to partition left no doubt about the probable result of that course of action. British representatives throughout the Arab world were in absolute agreement about the need to avoid further disasters in Palestine.

Even King George VI, a sovereign not renowned for his political opinions, recognised the errors of the past and remarked bluntly to Sir Miles Lampson, British ambassador to Egypt, that 'old Balfour was a silly old man; and had given (or promised to others) something already belonging to someone else!'[7]

Confusion regarding Palestine impacted directly on Arab policy. With no clear solution in sight, Britain lost its bearings in the region. The situation became so difficult to interpret that Anthony Eden, the foreign secretary, confessed in 1940 that Britain did not have an Arab policy because of the confusing complexities of Palestine.

The strike exacerbated tensions, and the mandatory authorities, clearly losing direction, embarked on a collision course with the Arab Higher Committee and the Mufti. They deported five members of the Committee to the Seychelles and dismissed the Mufti as its head. Under the Palestine (Defence) Order in Council of 1937, moreover, the high commissioner was given exceptional powers, and military courts were established in Palestine. These provocative moves led to the resumption of civil disturbances in October.

In desperation, Britain turned to King Abdel Aziz, as if, in doing so, a solution could be found. He was the one Arab ruler who was universally admired and respected by the British, and his importance to Britain was reiterated at every important decision point during the crisis. There were a number of reasons for this. First, he was the guardian of Mecca, and vital as such to the government of the largest Muslim country in the world (India). Second, his large kingdom occupied an important strategic position, connecting the Red Sea, the Gulf and India. Third, and equally important, he was a tall, proud and independent man with a commanding presence which fired the imagination and respect of all who came into contact with him.

Reader Bullard, the British minister to Saudi Arabia, denied that he was influenced by the 'noble Arab' syndrome, which had inspired so many other Englishmen. He claimed that his own high opinion of Abdel Aziz was not part of an illusion about the Arabs and that 'no Englishman who has lived within forty five miles of Mecca for five years could have any illusions about the "noble Arab" . . . No, my good opinion of Ibn Saud is . . . based on my experience of his actions for three years.'[8]

It is interesting to note at this point that an examination of British dispatches and reports from 1927 to 1953 reveals a persistent focus on Abdel Aziz, rather than on his country, by the different officials. It was the man and the king, rather than Saudi Arabia, who played a significant role in British policy considerations, almost as if the country was encapsulated in one man alone.

Throughout the 1936–9 crisis in Palestine, the Foreign and Colonial Offices sought to placate and obtain the approval of the king rather than the Palestinians. They conjured up solutions to the different crises with Abdel Aziz very much in mind. Because of their exceptionally high regard for him, and because he spoke unfailingly of Palestine, they anxiously sought his mediation at every possible opportunity. And they were willing at times to go even further to obtain his support: this included extending the borders of Saudi Arabia at the expense of British protected states.

Rendel argued against trying to 'buy' the king with inducements, since he was totally convinced it would not work. 'His strength lies in the consistency of his principles, and the support and respect of his people.'[9] Reader Bullard, who had long and first-hand knowledge of the king, echoed this conclusion. He agreed that Abdel Aziz would not respond to political bribes. 'What I am sure of is that nothing we can offer him would induce him to support the partition policy.'[10]

But London was at a loss on how to proceed. Regardless of the testimony of every Briton who knew Abdel Aziz that he could never be swayed regarding partition, a desperate attempt was made in December 1937 to do exactly that. For three years, the British government had been vigorously upholding the territorial claims of Abu Dhabi in the face of those of Saudi Arabia regarding the border areas between them.

In a surprising volte-face, however, the foreign secretary put forward a suggestion to his startled colleagues at a cabinet meeting in December. With the ultimate objective of inducing Abdel Aziz to accept partition, he discussed the possibility of conceding Khor el Odeid, which Britain had formally acknowledged as belonging to Abu Dhabi, to Saudi Arabia.[11] The India Office violently opposed this suggestion, on which no decision was reached immediately. It was not until the following year that the cabinet agreed to offer the ruler of Abu Dhabi £25,000 to give up Khor el Odeid.[12]

In early 1938, the BBC inaugurated its Arabic service.[13] To mark the occasion, Bullard went to Riyadh where the king would be listening with his court. As it turned out, the first item of the news bulletin in Arabic from London was about the execution of two Palestinians who had defied mandatory rule. The king burst into tears on hearing the news, and apparently remained upset for some time. The mortified Bullard reported later that the subject of Palestine was infinitely distressing to Abdel Aziz, who now dreaded listening to the radio. The king also emphasised to Lord Belhaven that no Arab would accept either partition or Jewish sovereignty.[14]

There can be no doubt that Abdel Aziz was in a quandary over Palestine throughout this period. On the one hand, he was a strong and steadfast British ally, and assiduously developed and relied on this relationship; and on the other, he hated what he saw as Britain's Zionist policy. Over and above this conflictual syndrome, Abdel Aziz feared more complicated reverberations. There can be no doubt of his personal feelings about Palestine. But he was also concerned about the fallout from the anti-British feelings that swept the Arab world and which could undermine his own relationship with Britain.

The astute Bullard had no illusions about the reasons for the Saudi alliance with Britain, never for one moment flattering himself that it was based on anything other than the king's innate expediency. He believed, for example, that the king had secretly provided arms and ammunition to the Palestinians.[15] 'The perfect friend', concluded Bullard, 'would ... have refused all help.'[16]

The king's policy of accommodating Britain was a function of his awareness of the limitations of his own power; he was very pragmatic and never reached beyond his capabilities. By the same token, Britain recognised the dangers of pushing Abdel Aziz too far because he represented a vital component of its Middle East policy. As the crisis deepened, the Foreign Office realised that Abdel Aziz's relationship with Britain was being put under very severe strain, and sought to contain it. The result was an uneasy alliance.

Abdel Aziz managed deftly to avoid taking official stands against Britain. He did not speak out publicly on his feelings about Palestine except to British (and, later, US) officials and representatives.[17] In fact, he had advised the Arab Higher Committee to cooperate with the Peel Commission, and had urged the Mufti to await its outcome before taking any action.

At the same time, he sent his personal recommendations and suggestions to the Peel Commission under four main headings: first, that Britain grant a general amnesty for all actions during the strike; second, that Jewish immigration be suspended for up to ten years; third, that land legislation be introduced to protect the small landowner from having to sell to the Zionists; and fourth, that Britain, along with the Palestinians, decide what kind of government should be set up there in the future.[18] It is worth noting that these would later be incorporated into the White Paper of 1939. The Foreign Office took the king's suggestions seriously, and commended them to the Royal Commission.

Once the Peel report was completed, the British government made elaborate arrangements to convey its contents to Abdel Aziz before they became public. This included flying out a copy of the text from London via Egypt on two RAF planes, and then to Jiddah, from where Bullard took them to Riyadh. The king therefore had twenty-four-hour advance knowledge of the text. He was totally opposed to its conclusions, and remained so throughout the coming months. But when Bullard made it clear that further discussion of the report would be unfruitful, the king, 'with his customary practicality of mind', did not talk about it any further at that meeting.[19]

In the following months, though, he continued to exert pressure on the British to alter their policy. At one point, his chargé d'affaires in London warned the Foreign Office that opposition to partition was very strong in Saudi Arabia. The Foreign Office privately refused to believe this because of the king's total control of his country, but it did concede that the most difficult question to decide was 'to what extent Ibn Saud was telling the truth when he professed to be embarrassed by pressure from the Wahabis and the ulema of Nejd'.[20]

Demonstrations took place in Jiddah, and a Central Committee for the Defence of Palestine was formed in Mecca with branches elsewhere in the kingdom. But the king would not hear of propositions by Palestinian and other Arab leaders that a conference to discuss the Peel report be held in Mecca.

He also refused to encourage any tribal gatherings to protest, although he did confess to Bullard that Britain's policy was disastrous to Britain and, ultimately, to himself. The British minister considered that the claim that the king's hand 'was forced to some extent by the violent opposition . . . [of Palestinian and other Arabs] . . . is doubtless true, but it is equally true that he detests Zionism and distrusts the Jews, and considers that, in giving way to these forces, His Majesty's Government are not only acting unfairly towards the Arabs but are compassing their own ruin, and therefore his ruin too'.

In January 1938, the Woodhead Commission was sent to Palestine to work out the details of the Peel recommendations. In the meantime, the enforced exile of the Mufti by the mandatory government left the Palestinians without effective leadership, which led to an increasing level of violence as the strike continued.

As he sought a solution, the colonial secretary, Lord Ormsby-Gore, was convinced of the vital role of the king of Saudi Arabia. He admitted to the prime minister that he considered Abdel Aziz to be the only Arab leader worthy of respect, and recommended: 'I think we ought to go as far as we can to secure—if necessary to buy—the friendship of Ibn Saud either financially or by territorial concessions.'[21]

He also considered the Saudi people to be the only Arabs 'of importance and value to us', and went on to say that 'the Levantine "Syrians" of Palestine west of the Jordan cannot by their makeup be much of an asset to anybody'.[22]

He was very much in favour of partition, and wanted Britain to be single-minded about promoting it, even considering the option of increasing Jewish immigration in order to create facts on the ground. Palestine was not just a local Arab problem, he said, but a world problem with repercussions in many countries.

The views of the colonial secretary had obviously been influenced and strengthened by the increasing difficulties of the mandatory authorities in Palestine. The continuation of the strike, the introduction of stringent military orders to combat the local resistance to British rule and the importation of British ex-convicts to reinforce the police all led to a deepening of the crisis.

In October 1938, the findings of the Woodhead Commission were complete. They concluded that partition would be impossible, and another solution had to be found. Almost immediately, a senior member of the Foreign Office suggested that the government abandon the concept of a Jewish national home, and that a Jewish state be found elsewhere in the British empire.[23]

The cabinet had earlier agreed that the foreign, home and colonial secretaries, along with the chancellor of the Duchy of Lancaster, should prepare a statement 'setting out the action which HMG proposed to take immediately with the Jewish problem'. At the cabinet meeting, there were suggestions that the Jews be settled in Kenya, Australia, Canada, Tanganyika, British Guiana or Northern Rhodesia.[24]

Although the Foreign Office was reconsidering policy, it had to contend with US pressure at a time when the Anglo-American alliance was vital to British security in case of a war. A bewildered British ambassador to Washington reported, for example, that President Roosevelt had suggested to him a scheme to solve the crisis in Palestine which would involve 'removing' 200,000 Arabs to make way for Jewish immigrants. It could be done, said the president, if the Palestinians were to be 'removed' to countries across the Jordan where water could be obtained with the help of US geologists through the boring of wells.[25] The Foreign Office dismissed the concept as ridiculous and reminded the ambassador that political interests and national sentiments could not be solved by economic sops.[26]

Once partition as a solution was thrown out, the next step to solve immediate problems was sought. In the light of the Bludan conference the previous year when Arab heads of state had met for the first time, the Foreign Office decided to invite representatives of the Palestinians and of neighbouring countries, as well as of the Jewish Agency, to confer in London on future policy, including Jewish immigration.

Preparations for the London conference were undertaken with one eye firmly fixed on Abdel Aziz. This was aptly expressed by the colonial secretary, who acknowledged that 'Ibn Saud's friendship would be worth more to this country than the friendship of any of the other Arab princes'.[27] The foreign secretary echoed this by stressing that the British government must make a determined effort to do justice to the Arab cause 'and more especially to conciliate our Arab friends and allies'.[28] In 1944, this was echoed by the minister resident in Egypt, who stated that 'Ibn Saud's attitude over the Palestine question borders on the fanatical, and he has assured me that he would, if necessary fight against the cession of any territory in Palestine to the Jews. You no doubt consider, as I do, that Ibn Saud is the most prominent figure in the Arab and indeed in the Moslem world today.'[29]

It is outside our scope here to discuss the conference, which took place in London in February 1939. It is relevant, however, to note the incorporation of Abdel Aziz's 1937 recommendations in the White Paper on Palestine which followed the meeting.[30] These included the establishment in ten years of an independent Palestinian state in which Arabs and Jews would share in government; the restriction of Jewish immigration for five years to no higher than 75,000, i.e. taking the Jewish population to approximately one-third of the total population, subject to the criterion of economic absorptive capacity; and that after the five years, no further Jewish immigration will be permitted without the express acceptance of the Arabs of Palestine.

A postscript to this period is provided by the beginning of the shift in importance of Palestine policy from Britain to the USA. A telling episode in the transitionary phase occurred in February 1945 when Abdel Aziz met Roosevelt at Great Bitter Lake, just north of Suez in Egypt. Roosevelt sought a meeting with the king for a number of reasons. Amongst these were an awareness of British esteem for the man (important in the context of the prevailing Anglo-American rivalry, which was especially acute at this time); the need to discuss economic and financial affairs; and the president's belief that he could use his personal charm and diplomacy to persuade the king to support a Jewish national home in Palestine.

Roosevelt had been warned by his foreign policy advisers that Abdel Aziz would never compromise on Palestine.[31] A modern historian of Saudi–American relations has claimed that 'Roosevelt clearly overestimated his own personal charm and misjudged the strength of the king's convictions'.[32]

Abdel Aziz stood firm against all mention of a Jewish homeland, and recommended that the refugees from the Third Reich be given living space in the very countries that had oppressed and persecuted them.[33] He obviously convinced the president of the extent of his feelings on the subject, and demonstrated that he refused to budge from his stand. In the end, Roosevelt told his secretary of state that the US government would have to review its policy on Palestine. This went against his election promise to Senator Robert F. Wagner of 15 October 1944 in which he undertook to help to bring about the establishment of a 'free and democratic Jewish commonwealth' in Palestine.[34]

During the conversation, the president undertook to do nothing to aid the Jews against the Arabs or make any move hostile to the Arab people.[35] He re-confirmed this after his return home. In a letter to the king, the president reiterated his promise that the US government would take no decision with respect to Palestine 'without full consultation with both Arabs and Jews'; and that he 'would take no action, in my capacity as Chief of the Executive Branch of this Government, which might prove hostile to the Arab people'.[36]

It is now known that Roosevelt also reaffirmed his Zionist pledge to Wagner at around the same time. The conflict arising from Roosevelt's different statements reflect his confusion on the subject after he met with Abdel Aziz. The meeting obviously made a great impact on the president.

In fact, he is quoted as having told his secretary of labour, a close friend, after Yalta, that the reason the Middle East was so 'explosive' was its poverty, and that after the war he and his wife would go there with a system like that of the Tennessee Valley to put things right.[37] He is also said to have told his wife shortly before his death that once his term of office was over, he wanted to live in the Middle East.[38] The death of Roosevelt soon afterwards ended a discrete phase of US policy towards Palestine. The next president, Harry Truman, had a completely different attitude, which was to promote the creation of the state of Israel in May 1948.

THE ARAB–ISRAELI WARS AND THE GULF

During the years after 1948, the entire region was undergoing so much radical change that linkage with the Gulf took on a much more subdued pace. This was the period when many Arab countries began to acquire independence from the severely weakened France and Britain. In this period the Arab world was reeling from the shock of the establishment of Israel, despite more than a decade of protests and appeals.

Tenuous links occurred at this time between Israel and the Gulf of which most people were totally unaware, including the governments involved. In early 1951, a small amount of crude oil from Qatar was being regularly shipped around the Cape of Good Hope to Haifa in Israel for refining. The empty tankers then called at Tripoli in Lebanon for IPC oil to go to other destinations.[39] This was confirmed in a Foreign Office minute in 1953 when it recalled that Kuwait had joined Qatar in shipping oil to Israel in 1951, at which point Qatar stopped doing so entirely. In 1952, 268,000 tons were shipped, and 600,000 tons in 1953.[40]

The Foreign Office was uneasy about the political face it would lose if the Arab League found out about the illicit trade, especially since Kuwait had undertaken never to do so. King Abdel Aziz had insisted on written assurances from ARAMCO that it would not ship Saudi oil to Israel.

Although it seemed likely that the ruler of Qatar was unaware of oil shipments to Haifa, the political agent in Kuwait was not totally convinced that the same applied to Abdallah al-Salim. The agent concluded that the ruler's policy of turning a blind eye might change if the Arab League 'turned the heat on him'.[41] It was finally decided to stop the shipments at the end of 1953.

The Gulf states by now had attracted large resident Palestinian communities. The personal links between the two began to take shape on both

26 Palestine and the Gulf States

the human and professional levels. During the period leading up to their independence, the Gulf states were primarily concerned with the process of development that accompanied the windfall of oil incomes. The main political links with the Palestine problem occurred at this time in the northern Arab world: in Egypt, Jordan, Syria and Lebanon.

The tripartite attack on Egypt in 1956 gave rise to a further manifestation of the linkage when Saudi Arabia cut off oil supplies to both France and England.[42]

The connections that had been so important during the 1936-9 period resurfaced immediately and very dramatically after the 1973 Arab-Israeli war. This time, however, they were clear for all to see and define.

3 Iran and Suez, 1953–1956

Three events of great significance to the Gulf occurred in 1953 that were to have a lasting effect on the region. The first was in June, when the monarchy in Egypt was abolished. This brought Gamal Abdel Nasser one step closer to the centre of power. A few months later he became prime minister, and then president. His leadership of the Arab world was to revive the importance of the Palestine problem, linking it with anti-colonialism, Arab nationalism, independence and modernisation.

The second event was the Anglo-American conspiracy in Iran which resulted in the overthrow of the elected prime minister, Muhammad Mossadegh, and the reinstatement of the shah in August 1953. The CIA-led coup was undertaken with British participation, an acknowledgement by the USA of Britain's hegemony. Britain had in fact instigated the movement to remove the prime minister, who had nationalised Iran's oil industry, and to replace him with the shah, who was more willing to accommodate Western oil interests.

This early example of 'regime change'[1] marked the start of US interference in the internal affairs of a Gulf state and was by far the most daring US exploit in the region until then. It had a lasting impact on the political development of Iran, the resentment continuing to grow until the Islamic Revolution overthrew the shah in 1979. The anti-American policies that followed were a direct reaction to the US role in the infamous 1953 coup. In 1998, in recognition of the mistakes made almost half a century earlier, Madeleine Albright, the US secretary of state, apologised for US meddling in Iranian internal affairs: she did so by acknowledging the deep-rooted resentment of the intervening forty-five years.

The third event was the death of King Abdel Aziz in October 1953, and with it the passing of an era in the history of Saudi Arabia. It was a milestone in the Arab world, recognised as such by Nasser, who attended his funeral. The warrior pioneer, who had created the country and held it together for more than fifty years, was followed by his chosen heir, Saud. The new king lacked his father's wisdom, character and charisma. He was ill-equipped to lead the country's transformation from a remote desert kingdom into a modern state with a substantial oil income.

Saud and Nasser steered their respective countries into an alliance that was short and intense. In 1954, Saud made a well-publicised state visit to Egypt to make public the new alliance between the two men. The two leaders were diametrically opposed in character, in outlook, and ultimately in national and foreign policy. One man was a traditional monarch, the other fiercely republican. One was dissolute, the other ascetic.

Yet their mutual interests drew them together at first. They were both strongly opposed to the 1955 Turkish–Iraqi treaty (precursor of the Baghdad Pact), which was a major catalyst in the Arab world, polarising regional alliances in a form that was to dominate politics for the next fifteen years. Nasser regarded the treaty as anathema to an independent Arab foreign policy; he viewed it as an insidious neo-colonial force which would disrupt the Arab world. Saud saw it as yet another attempt by his traditional rivals, the Hashemites, to dominate the Arab world; Iraq was ruled by the Hashemites, as was Jordan, which was considering becoming a party to the treaty.

Nasser's reaction to the treaty was to initiate Arab defence treaties to counter Iraqi reliance on Western security. The Saudi–Egyptian treaty (October 1955) was one such agreement. The two countries were now committed to Nasser's policy of positive neutrality, and Saudi Arabian money financed the publicising of this policy. The popular Egyptian radio station Voice of the Arabs, which reached almost every corner of the Arab world, owed much to Saudi money. Saud in effect financed the voice of Arab nationalism.

Another common interest of Nasser and Saud was their attitude towards Palestine and the need to redress the inequities of the situation. Egypt and Saudi Arabia were also united in their attitudes towards Britain. British forces were still in Egypt when Nasser came to power, and he quickly set about negotiating their evacuation, which finally took place in 1954. Lingering anti-British sentiments in Egypt were transferred to British control of other parts of the Arab world, such as Iraq, Aden and the Gulf states.

Saudi Arabia at the time was in direct confrontation with Britain over Buraimi—the crisis over territorial boundaries between Saudi Arabia, on the one hand, and Qatar, Abu Dhabi and Oman, on the other. The genesis of the problem went back to the 1930s, soon after Saudi Arabia signed its first oil concession. In order to define the geographical limits of the concession, the Saudi government sought to formally define its boundaries with the British-protected states on its eastern borders.

Anglo–Saudi conversations to delimit these boundaries first took place in London in 1935. Because Britain controlled the foreign relations of the Gulf states, it negotiated on their behalf. The 1935 talks resulted in a deadlock, and were resumed at different intervals during the next decade.

One of the main obstacles in resolving the problem was the differing outlooks of the Foreign Office and the India Office. The former was anxious to strike a compromise with Saudi Arabia, fully aware of King Abdel Aziz's pivotal role as a mediator in Palestine; it wanted to retain his goodwill and was willing to forsake tracts of land from the Gulf states to do so.

The India Office, by contrast, viewed the situation from the vantage point of the Gulf and British control of the region. It was aware of the growing influence of Saudi Arabia in the inland areas, away from British officials, and wanted to put a stop to its quiet but steady influence, which threatened the British hold on the region.

The different attitudes of these two departments ultimately resulted in a stalemate. This inaction meant that the dispute was placed on the back burner, particularly when the Second World War began. The tensions were not scaled down, however, and in 1949, they erupted. The US oil company SoCal (later ARAMCO), acting on behalf of Saudi oil interests, had started exploratory work in some of the disputed areas. The British government protested, claiming that the oil company was working in land that belonged to Abu Dhabi. Diplomatic efforts to resolve the dispute amounted to nothing, both sides standing firm in their claims.

In 1952, Saudi Arabia sent an armed force to one of the seven villages in Buraimi, the inland oasis claimed by Abu Dhabi and Oman. That was the beginning of the long and bitter dispute known as the Buraimi crisis. Britain sent in armed forces to counteract the Saudis, and a military stalemate froze the situation. Both parties then decided to initiate further diplomatic talks in an attempt to resolve the issue, on the understanding that all military action in Buraimi would cease pending the outcome.

Both sides withdrew to present written testimonies to an international tribunal. As a basis for decision, they detailed tribal loyalties, past and present, and their influence on the jurisdiction of Buraimi. But in the wake of dramatic mutual accusations by both sides, the proceedings broke down. Military action was resumed in late 1955, when British forces expelled the Saudi contingent still based in Buraimi.

The British government then claimed that three of the villages in the Buraimi oasis belonged to Oman and the remaining four to Abu Dhabi.[2] Saudi Arabia refused formally to acknowledge the rights of Abu Dhabi and Oman in Buraimi. Moreover, the entire question of the eastern boundaries of Saudi Arabia—that is, with the British-protected Gulf states—was to become a major cause of dispute and distrust until well after the 1970s. In the mean time, Saudi Arabia held Britain responsible for these territorial disputes, and remained unwilling to compromise with Britain.

So when Saud succeeded his father in 1953, Buraimi was still tense, Saudi soldiers were posted there, and Anglo–Saudi relations were at an all-time low. Abdel Aziz's long and smooth relationship with Britain was all but forgotten. Britain was more jealous than ever of its position in the Gulf, despite the dissolution of the British government of India. Its officials now were recruited from the Foreign Office. One of their main objectives was to protect British interests, particularly against Arab nationalism. Egypt and its allies, such as Saudi Arabia, were viewed with great suspicion.

Saudi Arabia's antagonism to Britain struck a resonant note in Egypt, where the Voice of the Arabs spoke for the Arabs, struggled for them and expressed their unity. Its broadcasts, which advocated Arab independence, Arab unity and Arab brotherhood, were widely listened to throughout the Arab world. Egypt and Saudi Arabia were in the nationalist, revolutionary camp of the Arab world, together with Syria and Yemen. Iraq was soon isolated, particularly after Jordan and Lebanon rejected the Baghdad Pact when popular movements expressed their opposition.

After Nasser attended the Bandung conference of non-aligned states in early 1955, his position in the Arab world was greatly enhanced. For the first time, an Arab leader was acknowledged and respected by such men as Tito, Nehru and Chou. Another milestone was the conclusion of the 1955 Czech arms agreement which underscored Egypt's position as a non-aligned country, free of Western influence. In reality, however, Nasser had repeatedly approached both Britain and the USA for arms, but had been consistently refused.

Nasser was acutely aware, as were his generals, of the urgent need for modern armaments, especially after a massive Israeli raid on Egyptian-controlled Gaza in February 1955 had killed thirty-eight Egyptian soldiers. Unable to defend themselves against the Western-trained and supplied Israeli forces which continued to launch devastating raids into Gaza, his officers appealed for a revamping of the army. When the USSR offered to help Egypt, he accepted after receiving yet another US refusal. In the growing Cold War environment of the time, with the war in Korea at its height, Egypt was regarded by the USA and Britain as being part of the Soviet bloc.

On the national level, Nasser also wanted Egypt to become economically self-sufficient. The Aswan Dam would not only provide irrigation to a vastly increased agriculture, it would also become a much-needed source of energy. The World Bank, together with Britain and the USA, were willing to help in the construction of the dam, but Nasser refused to accept the many conditions attached to the offer, afraid of dragging Egypt back into dependence on the West. Convinced that Nasser was at the same time negotiating with the USSR, America and Britain suddenly pulled out of the negotiations, along with the World Bank.

Nasser's response is well known. He nationalised the Anglo-French Suez Canal Company. Britain and France, incensed at what they considered the usurping of their inalienable right to the canal, then prepared the ground for an attack on Egypt. In a startlingly similar approach to the 1953 coup in Iran, they plotted another conspiracy: Israeli forces would launch the initial attack on Egypt, and the British and French armies would enter the fray, ostensibly to separate the Israeli and Egyptian forces, but in reality to occupy the Canal Zone. The Suez war began in late October 1956 with the Israeli invasion of Sinai, and a week later the British and French forces landed in Port Said.

In Britain, where the agreement with Israel was kept secret from all but a small group of government officials, a run on sterling obliged the prime minister, Anthony Eden, to turn to the USA for support. But America, angered at the entire war, refused Britain any help. Britain could not continue the course without US approval and financial support. Two days later, Britain and France had no choice but to back down and evacuate their forces from Egypt. The Israeli evacuation of Sinai followed a few weeks later at US insistence.

REACTIONS IN THE GULF

In Kuwait, the people were angered by the triple aggression on Egypt. The political agent admitted to the Foreign Office that the war had inflicted serious damage on British prestige. Feelings continued to run high, and in early December 1956 some sabotage to Kuwait Oil Company installations was reported. There was little other physical damage to British interests in Kuwait.

The other small states were relatively quiet, despite their anger at Britain's central role in the Suez debacle. Reactions, however, were muted and generally well contained except in Qatar. There the ruler, Ali bin Abdallah, assured the anxious political agent that his government would protect the lives and property of all people and companies in the country.

Ali was not slow to condemn British participation in the war. Although knowledge of Britain's collusion with Israel was still unknown, the ruler expressed his anger about the attack on a fellow Arab state on the first day of hostilities. The next day, all shops in Doha remained closed as a sign of protest against the attacks. Workers in the oil company went on strike and pipelines were cut at Umm Baba, not far from the refinery. They were repaired the following day, so oil production was not seriously affected.

The next day, people gathered together to protest and demonstrate against the attacks on Egypt. They were led by Shaikh Hamad and Khalifah al-Atiyah, a notable of Qatar. The following day a general strike was declared throughout Qatar. The ruler refused to export Qatari oil to Bahrain as a sign of protest against Britain. More than two hundred of his citizens volunteered to serve in the Saudi army which was to be sent to Egypt. Although the ruler did not encourage them to enlist, he did not discourage them from joining. The political agent reported that the ruler and every Arab he knew had condemned Britain's attack on Egypt. It was lucky though, he added, that Suez and Palestine are far away from Qatar and this had tempered the violence of feelings.[3]

A few days later, the political agent heard on the BBC radio that Syria was receiving Russian arms. He decided to visit the ruler and warn him to check enthusiasm in Qatar about these arms. The ruler turned on the political agent and asked him who was responsible, as Britain, which had created

Israel, had forced Egypt to acquire arms. He suggested that Britain put an end to Israel, which it created without the agreement of the Arabs.[4]

REACTIONS IN SAUDI ARABIA

In Saudi Arabia, to which Nasser went in a month before the attacks on Egypt, there was as much, if not more, popular support for the nationalisation of the Suez Canal Company. In the run-up to the war and soon after Nasser's visit to Saudi Arabia, a group of senior US officials visited the kingdom. They included Robert Anderson, former deputy secretary of defence, and Wilbur Eveland, CIA adviser. They had been sent by Eisenhower, who had been convinced by Howard Page of the Exxon oil company that Saud held the key to the solution of the Suez crisis. The delegation were joined by the US ambassador, and met with Saud and his advisers, including Crown Prince Faisal. Their mission was to persuade Saud to influence Nasser to accept foreign control of the Suez Canal Company.

They argued that unless Nasser retracted the nationalisation, Saudi oil would become worthless and the well-being of the entire Arab world would be threatened.[5] They also intimated that the Russians would be the only winners, since the West would have no choice but to boycott the canal. Moreover, they warned that the USA would soon be able to supply Europe with nuclear energy, which would be cheaper and more convenient than Saudi oil.

The Saudi answer—undoubtedly influenced by Faisal, who had spent time researching the subject of nuclear energy as an alternative source of fuel—was not long in coming. He expressed his doubts about imminent US nuclear capabilities and riposted that the best way to keep communism out of the Arab world was for the USA to use its leverage to force Israel either to repatriate or to compensate the Palestinians. Otherwise, war was imminent, at which point only the USSR would gain. Eisenhower's mission to influence Saudi Arabia failed, once again because of the strong US alliance with Israel.

Once the Israeli, French and British forces began to attack Egypt, Saudi Arabia joined the rest of the Arab world in cheering Egypt on. It granted the equivalent of $10 million to Egypt in aid. It also severed diplomatic relations with both countries on 6 November, and banned oil exports there. Petrol queues in Paris and London formed as the boycott began to bite. The petrol shortages were short-lived, in no way similar to those that were to devastate most of the industrial world in 1973.

Saudi–American relations were at an all-time low. The kingdom had already been named a 'disruptive force in Western-Arab relations'[6] before the Suez war. Tensions had been running high, attributed by the Office of Intelligence Research (OIR) of the State Department to 'Saudi resentment at US support of the Baghdad Pact and continuing plans to conciliate the

Arab-Israeli dispute'.[7] In the same report, the OIR confirmed that 'Saudi Arabia is more emotional on the Israeli issue than any other country' and acknowledged that ' the Saudis would like to be in a position to force radical changes in the US policy towards the Middle East', concluding that ' so long as the regime remains in power, no significant improvement in relations between the US and Saudi Arabia is likely to come about'.[8]

The aftermath of Suez was a watershed for the Saudi relationship with Egypt. The polarisation of the Arab world brought on by the war drove a wedge between the two countries, which grew steadily over the following months. It culminated in the tacit acceptance by Saudi Arabia of the Eisenhower Doctrine, a US policy enunciated by the president in January 1957. Its main objective was to provide and promote financial and military aid to those Arab states that wanted to resist communism. It was a calculated Cold War ploy to weaken Nasser and isolate his policy of positive neutrality.

In January 1957, Saud embarked on his first state visit to the United States, where the government was hoping he would accept the Eisenhower Doctrine. As his ship sailed into New York harbour, the king received a chilly and hostile reception. The mayor of the city ignored him and refused to extend even the most basic and simple of courtesies. He apparently acted out of deference to the large Jewish population of New York, who accused the king of being anti-Semitic.

At the same time, the federal government extended the warmest possible greetings to the king. The president, unusually, met him at the airport when he arrived in Washington DC later. Eisenhower and his government took great pains to offset the snubs of New York and at the same time to convince the Saudi leader of the merits of the Eisenhower Doctrine.

Although Saud never came out unequivocally in favour of the Eisenhower Doctrine, it was generally assumed that he had done so, particularly in Egypt, where Nasser felt threatened. He regarded Saudi Arabia as having deserted the neutrality of the Arab stand against the West. Perhaps the refusal of Saudi Arabia to renew the Dhahran Air Agreement with the USA in 1957 was not known. The agreement had first been made in 1946 for five years, mostly as a result of British pressure. As a result, the US air force was granted special rights in the airfield, bringing the country unofficially under the US security umbrella.

On the renewal of the agreement for a further five years in 1951, the USA undertook to supply arms and military training for the Saudi army, and to help establish a navy and air force. The agreement was renewed again in 1956 when the USA undertook to provide economic and military aid of around $180 million. Saudi Arabia had been weakened economically by the Suez war. This caused friction within the Al Saud, because some princes wanted more in concessions from the USA. In 1961, therefore, Saud refused to renew the lease.

In June 1961, Saud wrote to President Kennedy explaining why relations between their countries were at such a low ebb. He strongly criticised

American support for Israel despite the problems facing the Palestinian people, and objected to the US position on the whole dispute. He told the president that the only basis for considering the question of Palestine was that the Arabs were the legal owners of the country and had a right to live there; Israel was a usurper and aggressor which the USA was helping.[9] Although he refused to renew the Dhahran Air Agreement because of the US attitude towards the conflict, he did renew the lease for the US Military Training Mission in Saudi Arabia.

Contradictions within the Saudi policy towards the USA lay in the character and perspectives of the royal regime. On the one hand, its place in the West's camp within the polarised Arab world, along with other monarchical and 'reactionary' states, meant that it was regarded as pro-American, and therefore part of the pro-Israel grouping. On the other, it kept classified its consistent attitude to the USA vis-à-vis Palestine, so this element was unknown.

In September 1957, shortly after Saud's visit to the USA, Crown Prince Faisal visited Eisenhower at the White House. Only seven people were present: the president; John Foster Dulles (the secretary of state); a member of the Near East Office of the State Department; the prince; the Saudi ambassador, al-Khayyal; Ahmad Abdul Jabbar, chief of Faisal's office; and Camille Nowfal, an interpreter.[10] Eisenhower assured the Saudi prince that the USA would never allow Israeli aggression against Arab countries. That commitment had been made in 1950, and was reiterated after Eisenhower assumed the presidency. It had again been made clear in 1956 when the USA made Israeli forces leave Egypt. Faisal told the president that Israel was a constant threat to the Arabs, and that it was responsible for all the troubles in the past. When Eisenhower responded by saying that the USSR posed the greatest threat to the world, Faisal reminded him that Israel was the greatest danger to the Arabs, although he recognised the international threat of the USSR. Faisal had been acutely conscious of the Israeli threat since the 1947 UN vote on the partition of Palestine. He had attended the session and was so furious at the outcome that he stormed out of the General Assembly when the resolution was passed.

Moreover, the sudden and immense wealth of the country—most of all, of its royal family—brought about a significant social change which was difficult to come to terms with in a rational manner. This sudden wealth also pushed the state into a major regional and international role for which it was ill-equipped. Saud had been chosen by his father because of his ability as a tribal leader; it had been said that Abdel Aziz had wanted Faisal to be the international statesman, and Saud the tribal leader, and thus avoid any problems once he died.

Faisal became prime minister and foreign minister at first, but his brother gradually pushed him out of these central jobs, assuming his roles. By March 1958, however, he was forced to officially restore Faisal to his former functions, thereby granting him authority to carry out internal reform.

But Saud continued to mismanage the kingdom. This led to dissatisfaction within the royal family and to a polarisation of opinion on the prerogatives of royal power. In October 1962, despite the urging of the *ulema* and senior members of the Al Saud, Faisal refused to oust his brother and take the throne. He did, however, agree to become prime minister and form a government; he also became commander of the armed forces.

Faisal announced a ten-point plan for reform. Promises were made at this time to issue a constitution, establish local government, form an independent judiciary and other reforms. He re-established diplomatic relations with Britain and France. Problems with Saud continued to plague the government and the royal family, and finally in November 1964, he was deposed and Faisal became king.

Saudi conflict with Egypt grew rather than abated with time. In 1962, civil war broke out in Yemen after the death of the imam and his succession by his son, Muhammad al-Badr. A *coup d'état* against him led by the leader of the royal guard, Abdallah al-Sallah, set the stage for a civil war which was to last for seven years. Egypt supported the republicans, Saudi Arabia the monarchists. When Egyptian forces arrived in Yemen, it was inevitable perhaps that a military conflagration between the two would follow. Both sides sought to internationalise the conflict. Faisal wanted the USA to intervene on behalf of Saudi Arabia, but the Kennedy administration was unreceptive; it regarded the revolution as nationalist, not as a communist threat.[11] Moreover, it regarded Saudi weaknesses and threats to its sovereignty as emanating from internal issues. Faisal obviously agreed and sought an end to his dispute with Egypt.

Within a year of his accession, he met Nasser in Jiddah to work out a ceasefire agreement. Although at first it seemed as if a compromise had been reached, especially after a Saudi–Egyptian-sponsored conference brought together both sides, this was not the case. Renewed fighting, this time with the involvement of the air forces of both countries, continued. Ex-King Saud, who was residing in Egypt, made a public show of his support for the republicans by bestowing money on them. It was not until the 1967 war that Egypt and Saudi Arabia gradually ceased their belligerent posturing; the latter emerged the stronger after the 1967 war, and Nasser had no choice but to accept that fact.

4 Impact of the 1967 War

The June 1967 war between Israel and the Arab states was a defining moment in the modern history of the Arab world. It shattered Arab illusions about the course and benefits of positive neutrality. It was a blow to Arab pride and prestige. It undermined the leadership of Nasser in an unmistakable and lasting manner. It resulted in the creation of a new problem, that of the Occupied Territories, and thereby in the fading away of the original problem of the creation of Israel.

A singular and outstanding outcome of the war was the shift in focus of Arab leadership away from Egypt and towards the Gulf. Saudi Arabia gradually became the acknowledged power. The other Gulf states also grew in importance, especially in the light of their immense natural and financial resources. The Gulf region became an important destination for Palestinians in search of employment after losing their homes and jobs as a result of the war.

By the same token, the war drew the Gulf states into the Arab world more strongly than any other event had done. Hitherto, they had remained on the periphery—geographically, culturally and, even in some ways, economically. But after the war the people of the Gulf shared with other Arabs the devastation of defeat, and were consequently drawn closer to them. The war aroused great feeling among literate and urban Arabs everywhere, more so perhaps in the Gulf, where the isolation of long years of British treaty relations was swiftly coming to an end.

Saudi Arabia's recently acquired status in international relations reflected the new importance of the Gulf. Diplomats and statesmen began arriving there to offer solutions to the ever-growing crises of the refugees, the occupied lands, the truculence and aggression of Israel and the disarray of the Arab world. It was at this time that the Department of State sought to separate the Palestine problem—now referred to by the US media as the 'Middle East problem' and the 'Arab–Israeli crisis'—from the Gulf. In fact, a senior State Department official later confirmed that this policy of separation was deemed successful.[1]

Almost as soon as the war was over, King Faisal issued an embargo on sales of oil to the USA. The cut-off lasted only a few weeks, and went almost unnoticed. There were a number of reasons for the failure of Saudi Arabia's attempt to utilise this 'weapon'. First, there was a plentiful supply of oil available internationally, and at a relatively low price. Second, US production of oil was still considerable, outweighing all known suppliers at the time in the Middle East; the plentiful reserves of Abu Dhabi, for example, were still unknown, and other discoveries in the Gulf were waiting to be made. Finally, the international supply of oil was controlled by the so-called 'Seven Sisters', oil companies which had not yet encountered the efforts of the Organisation of Petroleum-Exporting Countries (OPEC) and the Organisation of Arab Petroleum-Exporting Countries (OAPEC).

But Faisal was not one to leave the matter there. He was totally overwhelmed by the fall of Jerusalem, and was to remain steadfast in his objective of retrieving it for the Arabs and Muslims until the end of his life.

At an Arab summit which took place after the war in Khartoum, Saudi Arabia, Libya and Kuwait set up a fund equivalent to $378 million (Saudi Arabia donated £50 million, Kuwait £55 million and Libya £20 million making a total of £125 million) for the countries directly involved in the war.[2] Egypt and Jordan were desperately poor after the war, and this gave Faisal a new leverage over his old enemy. Nasser and Faisal finally agreed to withdraw from the Yemen war, with both sides pulling out their forces and resources.

The Saudi people were also deeply disturbed by the outcome of the war, and unhappy at the US position in the entire conflagration. When the fighting was at its height, just after the fall of Jerusalem, on 7 June, the employees of ARAMCO in Dhahran went on strike. They had received permission from the governor of the Eastern Province, Ibn Jiluwi, to hold a peaceful demonstration the next day.

Around a thousand people walked to the US Consulate General, smashing windows and cars. They tore down the US flag, and replaced it with a Saudi one. They went to the Dhahran air base, and systematically destroyed the homes and cars of foreigners as well as the offices of American Airlines. The police and army were visible to all, but they did not intervene in the outburst of anger.

Then matters took a turn for the worse: 300 students from the College of Petroleum and Minerals broke into ARAMCO camp in Dhahran where the employees lived, and overturned cars, damaging almost a hundred, and destroyed the contents of the ARAMCO president's house. The vice-president of the company rushed to see the king, who assured him that Saudi Arabia needed the foreigners and that they would be safe. The Americans and Britons living there were not, however, reassured. They turned to their diplomatic and consular representatives, hoping for guidance. US citizens were told to get ready for evacuation from the country, but at the eleventh hour the plans were changed and the expatriates stayed on.[3]

Over a year after the war, two senior US officials, Joseph Sisco (assistant secretary of state for international organisation affairs) and George Ball

(US representative to the UN) were sent to the Middle East by president Lyndon Johnson to breathe life into the UN mediation effort. Their mission to the Arabs was to urge them to be flexible and to accept direct negotiations with Israel. They visited Jerusalem, Amman, Beirut and Jiddah. While in the latter, they had a working dinner with Omar Saqqaf, foreign minister, and Rashad Pharaon, adviser to the king, and then went to call on the king.

Faisal spoke in very emotional terms about the Israelis, whom he tended to equate with communists—a strong indictment at the time, when the Cold War was at its height. He was unswerving in his commitment to Arab Jerusalem, and admitted that if Egypt or Jordan ever agreed to allow Israel to retain the whole city, 'he would feel bound to declare a holy war against the Israelis in which he would have the support of all Moslems'.[4]

He apparently said that he saw no objection to the notion of direct talks between Arabs and Israelis so long as they remained within the context of UN Security Council resolutions. This contrasted with Saqqaf and Pharaon's statement that UN Resolution 242 was unacceptable to Saudi Arabia, but that the Saudi government would not interfere with its implementation by the states directly involved. Resolution 242 had been accepted by all Arab combatant states except Syria, which wanted an Israeli pull-out in exchange for non-belligerency and acceptance of Israeli sovereignty.

Gunnar Jarring, the Swedish ambassador to the USSR, was appointed by U Thant, secretary-general of the UN, according to Resolution 242, which called for a UN representative to facilitate negotiations. When the Jarring Mission began, Faisal made it clear that he agreed with most of the resolution except for the part about Jerusalem. He had said that if necessary he would join in a jihad to Jerusalem and that if all died, they would at least have died honourably. The US ambassador, Herman Eilts, apparently told the king that the US government rejected the notion 'that Jews could wail just as well in Brooklyn as in Jerusalem'.[5]

Faisal was very much like his father had been before him. He told everyone who visited him about the injustices of Palestine, and wanted to convince all of the validity of his arguments. He also informed visitors of the realities of the situation, convinced as he was of a massive Israeli misinformation campaign which had warped the truth. When Governor Scranton of Pennsylvania visited him in December 1968, he did not mince his words and, as he was wont to do, focused on the Arab and Muslim character of Jerusalem.

Faisal was particularly angry with the US government. He found himself in the same position as his father. While he relied on the USA for his security, he totally disagreed with its Arab policy but had very limited leverage with which to influence the outcome of the crisis. He was incensed by US policy on Jerusalem. In the face of the unilateral Israeli decision on 27 June 1967 to incorporate East Jerusalem within its borders the Johnson administration took the position that "there . . . must be adequate recognition of the special interest of three great religions in the holy places of Jerusalem." The US neither condoned nor adopted any measures to dissuade the Israelis from proceeding with their extension of Israeli sovereignty over East Jerusalem. For example they abstained from voting on the six power Security Council resolution A/L527/Rev.1 dealing with the city of Jerusalem.[6]

Faisal was particularly bitter about the address that President Johnson gave at the State Department on 18 June 1967 on American foreign policy.[7] He also was at a loss to know what exactly the USA's plans and policy were on the problem.

REACTIONS IN KUWAIT

A few hours after the war started, martial law was declared in Kuwait. It was to remain in force until January 1968. Feelings ran very high. In a country where the people were still poor and had supported the Palestinians in a generous way, it was inevitable that the situation in 1967 would be remarkably tense.

The loss of Jerusalem, along with the massive Arab defeat, was a double blow to the Kuwaitis. Arab nationalism had a broad base in Kuwait, whose government had not felt threatened by the rise of Nasserism—particularly after 1961, when the Iraqi president had laid claim to Kuwait. Nasser reacted coolly to the claim, refusing categorically to support it. He made it clear that Arab unity, his declared objective, could only come about as a result of a democratic process, and could not be imposed by military or other oppressive means.[8]

After British troops landed in the newly independent Kuwait to prevent any Iraqi military intervention, Nasser pushed for their replacement by the armies of the Arab League states. Once that was accomplished, the amir, Abdallah al-Salim, breathed a sigh of relief. Kuwaiti sovereignty had been assured not only by Britain and most other Western countries, but also by the acknowledged leader of the Arab world. The many Palestinian expatriates living in Kuwait were welcomed and given jobs. The amir also enjoyed a good relationship with two leading opposition figures, the Arab nationalists Ahmad al-Khatib and Jasim al-Qatami. The climate was right for a constitution, which was promulgated in late 1962, followed closely by an assembly, which was elected by male suffrage. Kuwait was set on a course which was to place it in the vanguard of political life in the Gulf.

The Kuwaiti government reacted positively and swiftly: generous financial donations were made to the Palestinians, as well as to Egypt and other front-line states which had suffered losses during the war; and Palestinians from the West Bank arrived to take up jobs there. By now the total Palestinian population in Kuwait had grown to 400,000. After the Arab summit in Khartoum in September 1967, Kuwait undertook to donate to Egypt and Jordan £55 million per year. This amount was substantial, since Kuwait had lost £75 million that year because of the devaluation of the pound sterling, the currency in which its assets had been held.

Kuwaiti anger at the outcome of the war was directed not only at Israel, but at the USA as well, for having supplied Israel with weapons and intelligence and for having supported it on the diplomatic and economic fronts. Although there were some anti-British feelings at first, largely due to Britain's strong alliance with the USA and thereby with Israel, these began to subside within two or three months, but not before the National Assembly had sent a telegram of protest to the Speaker of the House of Commons in London.[9] Feelings remained high against the USA, as the main supplier and supporter of Israel.

Anti-American sentiments were openly expressed in the press on a daily basis. Evidence of continued US support for Israeli activities in the face of the enormous human and physical losses of the Palestinians incensed the Kuwaitis. The national cinema company operated a boycott of American (and some British) films. Even the broadcast of American television serials was drastically reduced.

The US embassy was startled by the extent of the animosity, and some members privately believed it had official backing. It may have been paranoia, but US officials thought that they were being kept at arm's length in their official dealings, and that unforeseen obstacles seemed to have been placed over the arrangement of appointments with embassy personnel, with customs clearance, etc. It was difficult to pinpoint these obstacles, but they seemed to be cropping up all the time when they had not existed before.

The British embassy in Kuwait reported that Abdullah Bishara, private secretary of the foreign minister and owner of the newspaper *al-Yaqza*, had been a personal friend of the US ambassador. Relations between the two stopped being close after Bishara revealed the contents of the ambassador's interviews with Shaikh Sabah al-Ahmad Al Sabah. Bishara's actions, like those of most other Kuwaitis, were based on his attitude towards US policy on Palestine.[10]

It was not only the people of Kuwait who felt strongly about the subject. Members of the ruling family also became involved. Shaikh Fahd bin Ahmad, younger brother of both the prime minister (and heir apparent) and the foreign minister, was devoted to the Palestine cause. He had participated professionally in the 1967 war when he served in the Kuwaiti army on the Egyptian front. After the war, he had wanted to do more than just donate funds, and volunteered as a member of Fatah, the fighting force of the PLO.

He fought with the PLO in Jordan in 1968, when he was wounded in battle. He also went to Lebanon with Fatah in November 1969. There he was arrested by the Lebanese government. He was quietly and discreetly asked to leave the country.[11] Although he had trained as a professional soldier, he left the military and focused his attention for the remainder of his life on sporting activities, including Kuwaiti Olympic teams. He was shot dead by invading Iraqi forces in August 1990 as he stood at the entrance of his brother the amir's palace.

British officials privately registered a caustic attitude to the subject almost immediately after the war started. Geoffrey Arthur, former political resident and now British ambassador, noted with some sarcasm that for the first time since they had achieved independence, 'the Kuwaitis could find an opportunity to show their true Arab mettle'.[12] Just before the war began, the foreign minister had summoned British and other foreign representatives and warned them that their governments should not interfere in the forthcoming conflagration, otherwise their interests in Kuwait would be stopped.

When, in late May 1967, a battalion of the Kuwait army flew to the Suez Canal Zone, Arthur reported that Kuwait had moved into the frontline of battle and could not resist adding that 'Syria herself could not have done better'.[13] The ambassador was unable to understand Kuwaiti feelings for Palestine, and remained aloof and sceptical about them. He dismissed Kuwait's announcement of a defensive war against Israel on the morning Israeli forces attacked Egypt as 'a piece of humbug required by the Constitution'.[14] He condemned the Kuwaiti official he dealt with most, the foreign minister, as 'more of an enthusiast than most', and concluded that the government operated on two levels. The first was one in which it was carried away by the excitement of Arabism, and the second was based on sober calculation.

Oil production and exports were halted on the first day of the war. The foreign minister explained to Arthur that Kuwait had had to take such steps, which were only temporary. He made it clear to the British ambassador that Kuwait still relied on the British government for its protection, as it had in 1961, and did not want to lose the good relations it enjoyed. Oil exports were resumed in early July.

There was a run on the banks, and in particular on the British Bank of the Middle East, during the first few days of the war. The banks closed for three days, and by the time they reopened, that specific crisis was over. Arthur breathed a sigh of relief: 'To all outward appearances we have emerged comparatively unscathed here.' He did acknowledge, though, that the Kuwaitis had lost confidence in Britain. 'Their ease of association with us ... has gone; we do not see them socially now ... I doubt whether things will ever be quite the same again.'[15] He surmised that Britain did not lose out commercially by the war. Its greatest loss was its popularity with the Kuwaitis, but he quickly added that Britain could live without being popular with the Kuwaitis. His assessment was that Britain and Kuwait had a great deal in common which inhibited extreme action.

In July, the Kuwaiti battalion returned from the Canal front in Egypt. It had lost nine men, all presumed dead. A few wounded men were still in hospital in Egypt.

The foreign minister told Arthur in July that no Arab would negotiate with Israel. Arthur replied that Israel would be there for a long time and it would be detrimental for the Arabs to go on ignoring it. The Kuwaiti retorted that although the Arabs could not throw out the Israelis, they had friends who could. Arthur thought he referred to the Chinese. The British ambassador rather drily remarked to London that it 'only remains for me to remark that Shaikh Sa'ad is as moderate as people go here'.[16]

With time, however, Arthur began to feel the reality of Britain's position as an ally of Israel and the USA: 'I do not think that our position in Kuwait will ever be quite what it was before the 5th of June, 1967.'[17] He finally admitted that Kuwait had always been sensitive to events in Palestine, and that 'this sensitivity has grown with her increasing involvement in the Arab world'.[18] For the first time, he seems to have understood the nationalist sentiments of the people and their government. 'In every crisis in Palestine we lose something here, and this time we have lost a lot.'[19] And he finally admitted that 'I have never felt so isolated, even in Cairo.'[20]

Succeeding British officials in Kuwait remained sceptical when reporting local feelings about Palestine. When for example Sam Falle presented his credentials as British ambassador to Shaikh Sabah al-Ahmad in early 1969, he told the foreign minister that he had worked with the United Nations Relief Works Agency (UNRWA) in Beirut. This, reported Falle, provoked the 'fairly standard Kuwait line on Israel'. And it did not stop there. 'The burden of his song was that the time had really come for the Americans to take some action' to put an end to Israeli aggression. Falle admitted, however, that the foreign minister was quiet and reasonable. 'I have noted ... that if I wish to discuss any subject other than Palestine I must give no opening for raising Palestine.'[21]

In June 1969, Israel protested to the Security Council that Kuwaiti armed forces in Egypt were supporting acts of aggression in the Canal Zone against the occupying Israeli army. Earlier that year, when the prime minister opened the new Hilton hotel, he gave a speech condemning Israeli expansionism and aggression. Around the same time, the Kuwait government protested against the sale of British arms to Israel, and there were a number of people advocating the severing of Kuwaiti links with Britain as a result of its support for Israel.

British relations with Kuwait continued to deteriorate on many levels— except of course the official, where efforts to maintain proper links were made. By 1971, the British ambassador admitted that he rarely saw the ruler during the course of the year apart from the initial fifteen-minute call and a couple of handshakes later on during the year.[22]

REACTIONS IN BAHRAIN

Bahrain reacted in a much more muted manner to the 1967 war. Although many of the people were horrified by the course of the hostilities, particularly by the occupation of the West Bank and Gaza, their response was on an individual rather than official level. It must be noted here that unlike

Kuwait, Bahrain was still in treaty relations with Britain, to which it had officially relegated its foreign affairs.

Besides being technically a British protectorate, Bahrain also was passing through a period of internal instability whereby its deep-rooted opposition movement was in open conflict with the government under the leadership of Shaikh Isa. The Al Khalifah were somewhat remote from the rest of the Arab world at this time, preoccupied as they were by their own socio-economic and political problems. Although they were subdued by the outcome of the war, they did not have an army to send to the front, as had Kuwait, they lacked the vast financial resources of their neighbour, and they were not as interested in pan-Arab issues.

In 1970, at the very end of the British empire, the Bahraini government complained to the political agent that it was worried about the large number of Palestinians coming through the country, which it found highly undesirable. It was difficult to stop them since many held passports from the Trucial states, but the ruler and his prime minister found it too dangerous to allow it to continue uncontrolled. The agent reported that they claimed, 'with shining insincerity', that it grieved them to take action which other Gulf states might find unfriendly to the Palestinians.[23]

There were around 125 resident Jews in Bahrain. They had gone there originally from Iraq, and were mostly merchants and owners of properties which they leased out. Arabic was their native language and most held Bahraini citizenship. The main impediment to their total integration into Bahraini society was the fact that they only married within their own religious community; otherwise, they were nationals and were regarded as such by the society. After the war, they became apprehensive, although there were only a few incidents.[24]

In 1968 the Arab Boycott Office in Damascus discovered that the Bahrain Flight Information Centre, operated by the UK Board of Trade (Civil Aviation Department) communicated with aircraft of the Israeli national carrier El Al passing through Bahraini airspace once a week on a flight from Tel Aviv to Tehran and Nairobi. The Bahraini government had since 1966 been pressing the UK to cut the links, which were officially severed in September 1968.[25]

But they appeared to have continued when, in the summer of 1969, the British air attaché in Tel Aviv was informed by London that the bulk of traffic between Lod airport in Israel and Bahrain was related to meteorological information in the Gulf. Since that information was broadcast from Cairo and Cyprus, these links should be stopped.[26]

REACTIONS IN MUSCAT AND OMAN

Reactions to the 1967 war in the sultanate were very muted. There were no demonstrations, no overt hostility to Britain and the USA, no boycotts were declared, and there was only minimal evidence of Arab nationalist influence. Of course, local conditions were still very primitive indeed, and Sultan Said kept a tight rein on activity of any kind.

The British consul-general explained the muted response to the war. He found four reasons for it. First, it was partly due to the inward-looking nature of the country; second, it was partly because of the absence of other Arabs, including Palestinians; third, it was partly because of the lack of urban concentrations; and finally, partly because the sultan had shown so little interest in the subject.[27]

REACTIONS IN QATAR

By contrast, reactions in Qatar were heated and emotional. People in the main towns of Doha and Wakrah remained glued to their radios and TV sets, eagerly awaiting news of the battles, hoping against hope for Arab victory. The full scale of the defeat finally hit home by the end of the fateful first week of hostilities.

A dangerous situation arose on the night of 9 June, shortly after Nasser offered his resignation, which was broadcast all over the Arab world, and drove home the full extent of Arab defeat. It also underlined the feeling of loss experienced throughout the Arab world, which now became leaderless as well as defeated. The police force in Doha, along with their fellow citizens in the remainder of the country, had been shattered by the abrupt ending of their dreams of glory. A situation bordering on mutiny took place inside the police fort of Doha. The police force broke down and wept, in almost its entirety. The political agent rather scornfully claimed it was because of the 'downfall of their god'.[28] What was described as hysteria quickly swept the fort, and the situation threatened to get out of hand. The retainers and Bedouin belonging to the crown prince, Shaikh Khalifah bin Hamad, were called in to restore order. Calm returned before long, and the situation was never reported in the local press. Elsewhere, as in 1956, there was sabotage to the QPC pipelines and a well-head.

The government announced an embargo on oil exports to the UK and the USA on 20 June 1967, and refused to load tankers flying the flags of either of those two countries. The embargo was lifted on 5 September 1967.

REACTIONS IN THE TRUCIAL STATES

In the Trucial states, as in Bahrain, the reactions to the war were muted in view of the general preoccupation with internal affairs. The Trucial states were still comparatively poor. Shaikh Zayid of Abu Dhabi had been in power for barely a year, and there was much internal reorganisation still ongoing. This state of flux was echoed in the other states to different degrees and for different reasons.

Shaikh Zayid himself had not yet taken on the role he was to assume in the next decade as one of the wise pan-Arab rulers of the region. He was still very much a Bedouin leader, a man of the Buraimi oasis where he had started his political career. His outlook was parochial and quite limited in scope. Before the 1967 war he too had listened to the broadcasts of the Voice of the Arabs from Cairo, which used to attack the oil princes of the Gulf and label them useless and colonised.

He was wary of Nasser's influence in Abu Dhabi, and careful not to have a high profile in case it brought on an attack from the Voice of the Arabs. He admitted to the political agent that Nasser was the darling of the Arab world, and that every Arab ruler had no choice but to fall in behind him.[29] Accordingly, he sent a representative to the Baghdad oil conference, which took place right after the end of the war to discuss the stoppage of oil exports to the UK and the USA.

Zayid was totally overwhelmed by the scale of Arab losses during the war. He was very concerned about the sufferings of the Palestinians as a result of the war, and felt great sympathy at the loss of so many Egyptian, Syrian and Jordanian soldiers. Setting a pattern with which he later became associated, he immediately sent £1.3 million to Jordan.

The other Trucial rulers were even more removed than Zayid from the realities of the war. Shaikh Rashid bin Said of Dubai asked the political agent to provide him with a confidential analysis of what Britain perceived as the true causes of the conflict, obviously not totally sure himself.

When the hostilities started, demonstrations took place on the streets of Abu Dhabi. They were generally peaceful, and no damage whatsoever was reported.

In Dubai, by contrast, serious rioting broke out on 7 and 8 June, which the political resident described as having been 'led by Palestinians and exploited by hooligans'.[30] There was extensive damage to property, including British companies, but there were no serious personal injuries. The scale of the rioting took the authorities by surprise, as they had not been expecting so large a turnout. The political resident attributed the troubles to the encouragement of the Kuwait State Office, an old bogey of the British authorities; since the early 1960s, they had viewed its actions in the Trucial coast with much suspicion, concerned that it was yet another proxy of Nasser in the Gulf.

The Trucial Oman Scouts were called in, and restored order in a relatively short time. But that was not to be the end of the incident. Two Arab officers of the Scouts resigned as a result of the war. They did not want to be associated with a British military outfit at a time when Britain was regarded as having been a part of the attack on the Arabs.

In Sharjah likewise there were demonstrations, and some minor acts of sabotage. The British radio station Sawt al-Sahil was attacked and radio cable was cut. In neighbouring Ras al-Khaimah, the demonstrations were also large and very spontaneous. There was little damage reported, although stones were thrown around. In Ajman, Umm al-Qaiwain and Fujairah there was little if any response on a public level.

In conclusion, the 1967 war had a considerable impact on the Gulf states. In the independent states, the effect was obvious; while in those that were still bound by treaty relations with Britain and therefore more isolated from the rest of the Arab world it was latent in the sense that although it appeared muted at the time, there was a reaction that was to grow in strength rather than decrease.

The war's most important outcome was the entry of the Gulf into the Arab world. Hitherto it had been of little interest as a focal point. A glance at travel to and from the Gulf after June 1967 provides a strong indication of the shift towards this previously remote corner of the Arab world.

The Arab–Israeli problem was thenceforth shared by the countries of the Gulf, previously excluded. It became a central feature of the internal and external politics of the region. The political resident was astute enough to realise this almost immediately after the war. 'The maintenance of stability in the Gulf area, with our help, remains as important as ever,' he began. But he then acknowledged that this had now become 'more dependent than previously on our pursuing a policy in the northern part of the Arab world acceptable to the Arabs as a whole'.[31] This was perhaps the first overt official British acceptance of the integration of the Gulf into the Arab world.

The US government, by contrast, refused to accept this connection, although it acknowledged its existence. It sought instead to separate the issue of Palestine from that of the Gulf, in its broader Middle Eastern policy. It was only able, however, to separate the two for four years. In steadfastly refusing to acknowledge the linkage during these years, it revealed a short-sightedness which was to cost it dearly in 1973.

5 The 1973 Arab-Israeli War and the Oil Boycott

The two landmark Arab–Israeli wars, 1967 and 1973, were separated by six years—years that saw profound strategic changes in the structure of the Arab political and social environment. Although many of these changes were inherently local and national in origin, they were undoubtedly influenced by events well beyond Arab regional borders. The impact of international affairs during these years was universal as the Cold War intensified and the war in Vietnam saw an increasingly desperate US administration resorting to covert military operations and deepening involvement in South East Asia.

By the late 1950s the Gulf states had attracted large numbers of Palestinians, who were arriving to work and participate in national development. One of them, the poet Kamal Nasser, wrote a short poem extolling the virtues of Arab, Kuwaiti and Palestinian nationalism which he set to the music of the German song 'Lili Marlene' during the early 1950s.[1] The personal links between the people of the Gulf and the Palestinians had begun to take shape on the human and professional levels, as shown in Nasser's lyrics.

Throughout the 1960s, the Gulf states were primarily concerned with their own socio-economic development, which had remained stagnant throughout the period of British control.[2] During this time, it was in the northern Arab world—in Egypt, Jordan, Syria and Lebanon—where the main links with the Palestine problem occurred, mostly on the political level. The Palestinians had no formal political representation in Arab and international organisations, and relied on these countries to act on their behalf.

The beginning of a new period, one in which the Gulf became directly linked with the problems of Palestine, started in early 1968 when the Labour government in London announced its withdrawal from all its bases east of Suez by 1971. This included of course, the Gulf states, most of which had been in treaty relations with Britain since the 1820s: Bahrain, Qatar and the seven Trucial states.

The announcement of withdrawal was sudden and without warning, and for the following three years, the rulers of these states were engaged in meeting after meeting, discussion after discussion, plan after plan, to decide on the political shape of their future without British protection. There were many problems. Bahrain had the largest and most educated population; it was, however, relatively poor, especially when compared with the enormous wealth of Qatar and Abu Dhabi. The latter had only just started the process of modernisation: Shaikh Zayid bin Sultan (1966–2004) had replaced his brother Shakhbut bin Sultan (1928–66) as ruler only two years earlier, and immediately set the wheels in motion for rapid development, thanks to the enormous income from the sale of oil.

Before the shock of Britain's announcement of withdrawal had had time to take effect, Zayid sought an arrangement to provide an alternative form of security for the small states. He met Shaikh Rashid bin Said of Dubai to settle a long-standing offshore dispute, and shortly afterwards the two rulers announced the formation of a federation between their two states. They invited the other states to join.

Although willing at first to consider joining the federation, Bahrain and Qatar ultimately opted to go it alone. That left the seven Trucial states. Of these, Abu Dhabi undoubtedly had the greatest power, both because of its great wealth and Zayid's leadership abilities. The United Arab Emirates (UAE) was established in 1971, with Shaikh Zayid as its president, a position he continued to hold throughout his life, and Shaikh Rashid bin Said (1958–1991) of Dubai was named prime minister.

In December 1971, Britain, which had dominated the Gulf for 150 years, left the area permanently. The political resident lost his empire, as four new Gulf states became independent.[3] The political structures established by Britain over the long years could not remain static forever, and were vulnerable to the forces of change. On the eve of withdrawal, Iranian forces seized the three islands of Greater and Lesser Tunb and Abu Musa, claimed by Ras al-Khaimah and Sharjah respectively and recognised by Britain as such during the period of its rule there.

The British government had been forewarned about the imminent occupation of the islands by the shah before withdrawal. This fact only became known recently, when the official documents pertaining to that period were declassified at the National Archives in London. Until then, Britain had officially feigned ignorance of Iranian plans, and expressions of surprise were followed by public attempts to restore the islands to their rightful owners.

Throughout the period of negotiations regarding the forthcoming independence of Bahrain and Qatar, Saudi Arabia felt that it had been bypassed and outflanked by Britain and Iran. It wanted a say in the establishment and future of the UAE. One way of expressing this was in upholding the rights of Sharjah and Ras al-Khaimah over the islands.

Saudi Arabia was primed to become Britain's successor in the Gulf states. It readjusted its policies towards them accordingly, particularly regarding the various border disputes it had had with them since 1913 when it had first extended its power to Hasa. Its attitude was now governed by the new dynamics of the region. With its increased stature, it functioned on two levels: that of its relationship to the entire Gulf region, including Iraq and Iran; and its relationship to the Arab world as a whole.

It gradually drew its mantle of protection over the Gulf states, and viewed its relations with them as part of a wider regional perspective. In early 1973, for example, Iraqi forces occupied a Kuwaiti police post and refused to withdraw; fighting ensued, resulting in a number of wounded and killed on both sides. While the Arab League intervened to mediate, Saudi Arabia acted to maintain the status quo.[4] It quietly and temporarily dropped previous claims it had made to islands in the Kuwait area, and defended Kuwait against Iraqi moves. Saudi Arabia thus replaced Britain in seeking to consolidate the established territorial order of the region.

In the meantime, the USA was actively seeking the establishment of a new security system in the Gulf to fill what it regarded as the 'power vacuum' resulting from Britain's departure. Its primary motivation at that time was the fear of Soviet encroachment on what, because of its economic importance, had become a vital region to western industrial countries. The Nixon administration therefore formulated what became known as the 'twin pillar' policy: reliance on both Iran and Saudi Arabia.

Of the two, Iran was militarily more capable of securing Western interests. The shah was given almost unlimited US military and intelligence assistance, and gradually came to be regarded as 'the policeman of the Gulf'. As military aid of all kinds arrived in astonishing quantities from the USA, the ambitions of the shah grew correspondingly. He was provided, for example, with covert CIA and Mossad aid to help the Kurdish revolt against the central government in Iraq; this gave him great leverage over Iraq and enabled him to impose the Algiers agreement whereby Iraq conceded part of the Shatt el-Arab waterway to Iran in 1975. This was to become one of the causes of the Iraq–Iran war that started in 1980.

Saudi Arabia, the pillar that was considerably weaker than its 'twin', was regarded as the stabilising influence on the smaller Gulf states. US support therefore enabled it to enhance its position in the Gulf region, and ultimately throughout the Arab world. The USA did not go far beyond this level of support, in strong contrast to its provision of a vast arsenal of weapons and intelligence to the shah. King Faisal was acutely aware of these differences, and made his resentment known to British and US diplomats and other officials. While not impervious to the king's complaints, the US government did little to alter its twin-track approach, convinced of its long-term validity.

THE GULF CLOSES RANKS

But a new dynamism, which US policy had not taken into account, had entered the Arab world. It was registered in a closing of ranks and extended to all countries—poor and rich, small and large, conservative and progressive alike. The festering problem of Palestine had grown substantially since the June 1967 war. It was of great significance in Arab consciousness and the nub of political life. The political resident in the Gulf had recognised the impact of Palestine throughout the region since 1967, admitting then that stability in the Gulf was dependent on British policy in Palestine.[5] This admission, like so many others by Western officials, diplomats and statesmen over the years, was ignored with determination and remarkable obstinacy by policy makers.

The general consensus in Western countries was that the sentiments expressed by such leaders as King Faisal were neither serious nor sincere. This was encapsulated in a 1970 report by the British embassy in Jiddah: 'On the Palestine imbroglio, the Saudis have continued to play their unheroic role, trying to keep trouble away from themselves, while privately praying for, and directly assisting, the frustration of the extremists.'[6] This constant in Western attitudes towards the Palestine conflict grew rather than abated with time, and has survived in one form or another until the present. It is reflected in the works of a number of Western or Western-based scholars who adopt the view that the governments of Saudi Arabia and other Gulf states use the Palestine problem with great cynicism to further their own ends.[7] This body of literature survives into the twenty-first century with remarkable insouciance and lack of evidence.

In 1969 a Saudi brigade was sent to Kerak in Jordan to support other Arab forces in the confrontation against Israel; one Saudi soldier was killed and several wounded. The next year, the situation in Jordan was radically transformed by the fierce civil war between the Jordanians and Palestinians, with substantial casualties on both sides. Jordan emerged victorious and the PLO was driven out of the country. The British embassy in Jiddah decided that Faisal was relieved at King Hussein's victory over the PLO; he had apparently resumed financial donations to Jordan quickly, all the while continuing to 'use the purse-strings to keep him [King Hussein] in the position of *demandeur*'.[8] The embassy also noted that Faisal simultaneously kept the lines of communication with the PLO and Yasser Arafat open.

Saudi Arabia's awareness of the increasing importance of its oil reserves directly affected its foreign relations. It realised the potency of oil as a weapon, which introduced a new activism into its relations with the West, and the USA in particular, as Israel's greatest supporter. The US government acknowledged the new international status of Saudi Arabia but was unable to foresee the use of oil-production levels as a lever for political objectives. In fact, as late as 28 September 1973, less than three weeks before the oil embargo was declared, senior State Department officials thought it unlikely that there would be any Saudi oil embargo during the course of that year.[9]

King Faisal became increasingly involved with Sadat and those African states that had indicated a readiness to sever ties with Israel. He was also developing relations with Fatah, the branch of the PLO to which Yasser Arafat belonged. In his new role as the acknowledged leader of the Arab world, particularly after the death in 1970 of Gamal Abdel Nasser, the king wanted to incorporate the Palestinian movement into the main body of Arab politics; he did not want it to remain simply as a guerrilla group. He wished the PLO to become a respectable organisation, one that could become part of conventional political life in the Arab world.

Faisal had grown in stature as an international statesman. The USA regarded him as a moderating influence in the region, the one Arab head of state who was successful in maintaining the initiative, not allowing Iraq or Syria to wrench it away. The issue of Jerusalem dominated his relations with the West, the USA in particular.

When in May 1971, William Rogers, the US secretary of state, visited Saudi Arabia to promote a new peace plan, the king responded by urging the USA to stand against aggressors who acquired territory from their neighbours with such impunity; and he was emphatically against Jerusalem remaining under Israeli control. He reminded Rogers that the Arabs had made concessions over and again, the Israelis never.[10] This message was conveyed to Washington many times but it was brushed aside. The reality of the US position was put forward by President Nixon's national security adviser, Henry Kissinger, to the British diplomat Anthony Parsons in June 1971.

Parsons had asked Kissinger for any help the USA could offer to change Faisal's attitude towards the West regarding the Palestine problem. Kissinger replied that the king had told Nixon on one of his visits to Washington that relations between their two countries would be greatly eased if the USA would arrange to return Jerusalem to the Arabs. Kissinger explained: 'The result had been that the President had lost the Jewish vote and gained three Arab votes.'[11]

The Saudi government was resentful of the USA's low-key response to their urgent requests for a fair solution. All the same, it continued to be a loyal ally. In late 1971, the US government had asked that Jamil Baroody, the Saudi representative in the UN, stop pressing the Political Committee for a draft resolution to ban nuclear tests; the USA found this embarrassing, and Baroody accordingly stopped. In a meeting with Bill Stoltzfus, the US chargé d'affaires in Jiddah, the Saudi minister of foreign affairs, Omar Saqqaf, spoke with extreme bitterness about the contrast between American efforts regarding the test-ban issue and their inadequacy in solving the Arab–Israel dispute.[12]

The Kuwaiti stance on Palestine during this period differed somewhat. While the amir and the upper echelons of government were more restrained in expressing opposition to Israel, the Kuwaiti people were vocal, and rarely shied away from blaming the USA. When Spiro Agnew, vice president of the USA, made a short visit to Kuwait in July 1971, the vibrant local press, which was strongly pro-Palestinian, viewed the visit entirely from the angle of the Arab–Israel dispute. One of the papers, the *Daily News*, alleged that the US ambassador, John Patrick Walsh, had said that Agnew's visit was for electioneering purposes; and that he had also said that the State Department was so 'over-plagued' with Zionist propaganda that it would not listen to him, with the result that he had considered resigning as ambassador. Walsh denied saying that, although he was known to be pro-Arab.[13]

The British were more sensitive to their position in Kuwait, and realised that they were being tarred with the same brush as the USA because of the strong alliance between the two states, and that Kuwait's historical ties with Britain were altering in the aftermath of the Arab wars with Israel.[14] Britain was paying for its 'special relationship' with the USA, which until 1971 had been one of great rivalry in the Gulf, an irony that was not lost on some of its officials.[15]

THE ROGERS PLAN

William Rogers, US secretary of state, introduced a new peace plan in late 1969. It was based on a compromise solution to the territorial dispute for which Israel had rejected Resolution 242. Once again, Israel refused this plan, and the Egyptian 'war of attrition' began soon after; it was intended as a means of forcing the Israeli army to maintain a permanent state of mobilisation around the Suez Canal area.

After Anwar Sadat became the new president of Egypt in September 1970, Rogers seized the opportunity once again to launch a peace plan. There had been serious Cold War implications of the conflict, with the USSR supporting first Syria and then Egypt, and the USA was keen to break the deadlock. Although he was regarded with considerable respect in the Arab world, Rogers at this time was becoming increasingly marginalised by Kissinger. This marginalisation worsened after the peace talks with China and Vietnam in 1970 and 1971. During that period, President Nixon had given Rogers scope to act vis-à-vis the Arab–Israeli dispute, but after he was re-elected in November 1972, this gradually came to an end.

Rogers initiated the concept of secret negotiations between Israel and Egypt, having sounded out Sadat on the idea. He was increasingly worried about the possibility of an oil embargo and a superpower confrontation on what had become the most intractable of international crises. This was made more acute with the signing of the Soviet–Egyptian treaty, followed the next year by the Soviet–Iraq treaty. But by then, Nixon, acting on Kissinger's advice, had told Rogers not to proceed with his initiative, which died a natural death soon afterwards.[16] In August 1973, Rogers resigned as secretary of state.[17]

A few months earlier, Faisal had sent his oil minister, Ahmad Zaki Yamani, to Washington to inform the US government that if it changed its pro-Israeli stance, Saudi Arabia would increase oil-production levels, thereby keeping prices low.[18] Oil production had already been increasing and, by July 1973, was 37 per cent higher than the year before.[19] The king was neither quiet nor secretive about this linking of oil policies with Palestine. He was particularly frustrated by the US veto of the UN Security Council resolution (S/10974) of July 1973 which deplored Israel's continued occupation of Arab territories. He gave numerous press interviews on the subject, one of the most memorable being in *Newsweek* magazine on 10 September 1973.

Faisal's attitude marked a significant change in Saudi policy. Barely a year earlier, he had indicated in a press interview that oil would not be used as a political weapon. A precipitating factor for the new dynamism was undoubtedly the July 1973 US veto; it was the only veto for a resolution deploring Israel's continued occupation of the West Bank and Gaza. The king was also annoyed by the continuing arms sales to the shah, the other partner in the 'twin pillar' policy, which were transforming the Gulf into a dangerously militarised zone.

THE OCTOBER 1973 WAR

The petering out of the Rogers plan was a major disappointment to Sadat, who sought a way out of the 'no peace no war' impasse. The deadlock was finally broken on 6 October 1973, when Egypt and Syria launched a co-ordinated pre-emptive strike against Israel. It became known as the 'Ramadan war' and/or the 'Yom Kippur war' because it occurred during both religious (Muslim and Jewish) festivals, depending on the side which made the appellation. Israel had feared an imminent attack, but had been warned by Kissinger against launching a pre-emptive strike, something Kissinger later denied having done on more than one occasion.[20] The Egyptian attacks began in the early afternoon, engulfing Israeli forces on the east bank of the Suez Canal; and at around the same time, Syrian forces broke through Israeli positions on the Golan Heights.

Sadat had already made it clear that his objective was a limited war to force the Israelis into accepting a compromise settlement to the problem that was paralysing the Middle East. The Arab armies at first achieved major advances, finally ending the concept of Israeli invincibility. The UN Security Council hurriedly called for a meeting to obtain a ceasefire. Abba Eban, the Israeli foreign minister, asked the USA to delay the meeting to allow Israeli forces to recoup their losses before the ceasefire.[21] Kissinger agreed, and duly deferred the UN meeting to give the Israelis enough time to recover. The recently released documents of the US National Security Council reveal the extent and variety of aid extended by the USA, mostly by Kissinger himself, throughout the conflagration; much of the US help was top secret, despite many public statements to the contrary. It was during this war that the linkage between the Gulf and the Palestine problem rose to the surface and dominated international affairs for several months.

At 8 a.m. on the morning of 9 October, the Israeli ambassador, Simcha Dinitz, told a stunned Kissinger at the White House that Israel had already lost 500 tanks and required military reinforcements of all kinds. 'I don't understand how it could happen,' commented Kissinger. 'Our strategy was to give you until Wednesday evening [10 October], by which time I thought the whole Egyptian army would be wrecked.'[22]

Another top-secret meeting at the same venue took place that evening at 6 p.m. when Kissinger informed Dinitz that Nixon had agreed to replace all Israeli losses, including tanks (M-60s, the newest available), aircraft (five F-4s), electronic equipment, etc. Any specific objections from the Pentagon regarding the secrecy of the mission were swept away by Kissinger, who made it amply clear to the ambassador during that meeting that the US government would help Israel in every way possible.[23]

The airlift was to be secret, but it was not long before news of it broke to an anxious Arab world. There was considerable Arab anger at such overt US aid to Israel; many inevitably raised the idea of using the oil weapon in self-defence. In Jordan, King Hussein announced the mobilisation of his army, explaining to the US ambassador that it was only a 'psychological act' to appease his large Palestinian population.[24]

Another top-secret meeting at the White House between Simcha Dinitz and Kissinger,[25] together with two of their aides, took place the next day, 10 October. Kissinger tried to reassure the ambassador about US support, and provided him with different options on how to overcome the impasse his country was facing. Making it clear that he was talking in his private capacity, he revealed that there was overwhelming pressure in the USA for the government to do something about the Arab–Israeli conflict, and that most people saw Israeli intransigence as the root cause of the problem. Dinitz expressed concern that Joseph Sisco, assistant secretary of state for Near Eastern affairs, was talking in terms of Palestinian 'rights' and not 'interests', and that the Arabs were linking everything with Palestine.

Kissinger explained to Dinitz that one strategic option for Israel would be to exhaust the Arabs by presenting them with many proposals, and at the same time never having to give up a key position—much as he had done with the Vietnamese talks in 1972. Another option would be to split the Arabs: 'We have to find a way of splitting the Arabs . . . We could try to split off the Saudis.'[26] Kissinger told the Israeli diplomat that three years earlier, oil company executives had gone to the White House asking for something to be done about Jerusalem. 'This won't be made as an American proposal; you can count on that. But it would help with the Saudis; this is the only thing they express themselves on. It would help domestically.'[27]

Kissinger made his attitude towards the conflict perfectly clear: 'My strategy is to keep the Saudis out of the Arab–Israeli dispute, because any settlement achievable wouldn't be satisfactory to Arabs, and it would only weaken the regime to have to take responsibility for it.' Kissinger had more advice: 'You must keep the Arabs on the defensive.' He continued: 'My strategy is to exhaust the Arabs. We have been doing it, but every time, some one of our people pops off . . . If we can figure out some way to split the Saudis off . . . Jordan is already split off. The Syrians won't be. But Egypt is already willing to make a separate peace.'[28]

Kissinger was to prove unable to split off the Saudis. The documents show that Faisal was furious when he heard about the US airlift to Israel. Kissinger blatantly alleged that the USA had only started the airlift after Soviet aid to the Arabs had reached massive proportions.[29] This he claimed in a communication to King Faisal on 14 October, four days after he had unconditionally granted the Israeli army all its requirements except for laser bombs.

The allegation that the USA only approved the airlift after the Soviets had sent reinforcements to the Arabs was reiterated at a White House meeting of four Arab ambassadors with Nixon and Kissinger on 17 October. The Arab ambassadors were: Omar Saqqaf, minister of state for foreign affairs, Saudi Arabia; Ahmad Tibi Benhima, minister of foreign affairs, Morocco; Sabah al-Ahmad Al Sabah, minister of foreign affairs, Kuwait; and Abdel Aziz Bouteflika, minister of foreign affairs, Algeria. Also attending were Joseph Sisco, William Quandt (staff of National Security Council) and Alec Toumayan, State Department interpreter.[30]

Omar Saqqaf did most of the talking on behalf of the ambassadors. Dignified and eloquent, he made it clear that all the Arabs wanted was a return to the 1967 borders and a respect for the right of return of the Palestinians. Nixon deliberately told the Arab statesmen that he had organised the airlift to Israel only in order to maintain the military balance after 300 Soviet planes had re-supplied Syria and Egypt.

It is difficult to assess with much accuracy how much information Nixon had had of the timing of the airlift, and whether or not he knew he was not being truthful in this interview. Telephone transcripts of the White House, recently released by the National Archives in Washington DC, indicate that he was decidedly off-centre during this period. He was, for example, too drunk to answer a phone call from Edward Heath, the British prime minister, that same day.[31] His vice president, Spiro Agnew, had resigned from office only one week earlier (on 10 October) because of a bribery scandal, adding to the personal and political problems he was facing. It can be assumed that the president was preoccupied with salvaging his position, and relied heavily on Kissinger for information and policy on the Middle East.

Kissinger was triumphant, convinced that he and Nixon had thwarted the use of the Arab oil weapon. He made fun of Saqqaf, saying gleefully after the White House meeting: 'Did you see the Saudi Foreign Minister come out like a good little boy and say they had very fruitful talks with us?' He concluded that 'we don't expect a cut-off in the next few days'.[32]

THREAT TO OIL PRODUCTION

He was wrong. The previous day, on 16 October, the Saudi deputy minister of foreign affairs in Jiddah had called in the representatives of the nine members of the European Community (EC). He wanted their governments to pressure the USA to be 'even-handed', otherwise Saudi Arabia would cut back oil production and urge other Arab oil-producing countries to do the same. The note given to the British ambassador after the meeting referred to the USA's recent pro-Israeli stance regarding arms reinforcements and that it would be up to the European countries to advise the USA to change its attitude, knowing they would be the most likely to be harmed by a cutback in oil.[33]

The British foreign secretary, Alec Douglas-Home, was panic-stricken. He instructed the embassy in Jiddah to contact King Faisal or any of the senior princes immediately and remind them that Britain had constantly promoted UN Resolution 242 and had urged the US government to do the same.[34] The British government was offended at the Saudi implication that it was doing less than it should towards a peaceful settlement, and that the threat of a disruption of oil supplies could make it work harder.

Britain and the USA had obviously misjudged the extent of Arab sentiment, particularly after early Arab military successes became known. They had a limited perception of Arab feelings about Palestine, most of all about the loss of Jerusalem in 1967. They were flailing around, Britain and the other European countries particularly, trying to find a quick solution to what they suddenly realised could become a major economic, let alone political, crisis.

The British ambassador secured an urgent meeting with Prince Fahd, who reassured him that Saudi Arabia did not want to damage European interests, but could not distance itself from the general current of Arab opinion. He urged Britain to organise an unequivocal European statement calling on Israel to withdraw to its 1967 borders, after which Saudi Arabia would be able to restructure its position regarding oil.[35]

Generally speaking, the governments and rulers of the Gulf states were angered by the support that the USA was openly providing Israel, and had an exaggerated view of European ability to influence the USA. Shaikh Zayid, president of the UAE, told the British ambassador that he was aware of the European predicament and promised to try to promote an 'increased offtake'.[36] He had earlier told him that he would not cut off oil to the UK and that he thought sanctions should be confined to countries helping Israel. Zayid was proud that the Arabs had achieved a common approach to the conflict in Palestine, and was determined not to throw away the opportunity to stand together. He was not totally supportive of all Arabs, however; he sharply rebuked Hassanein Haikal's article calling for an immediate use of the oil weapon, saying that Haikal was a journalist, not a policy maker. It was during this crisis that Zayid began to evolve from a parochial, tribal leader into a champion of Arab causes. The quadrupling of the oil prices during the following months struck home the powerful role he could play with his enormous financial resources and elevated his standing in the Arab world as a generous benefactor. His rebuke of Haikal was a reminder of his anti-Nasser feelings of the late 1960s when he and other Gulf rulers were attacked as corrupt and reactionary on Sawt al-Arab, an Egyptian radio station which beamed its broadcasts throughout the Arab world. After the death of Nasser and the focus of power on Saudi Arabia, most Gulf rulers were more relaxed about their relationship with republican Egypt.

In Kuwait, the prime minister repeated what other Gulf governments had expressed: they were reluctant to punish Europe and Japan for US policy. The prime minister went further and said he had no desire to harm the friends of Kuwait.[37]

The amir of Qatar, Khalifah bin Hamad, differed somewhat from his colleagues. He was much more outspoken in his condemnation of the USA and the endangering of its interests in the Arab world. He was bitter about the embarrassing position in which Nixon had placed Faisal by being so blatantly pro-Israel. Saudi Arabia and the other Gulf states wanted to show their solidarity with the rest of the Arab world. He regretted the harm this would cause their friends, but left it to them to influence the USA.[38]

Bahrain, which had no oil weapon to use, reacted in another way. It closed the US naval base in Jufair, and cancelled all its facilities.[39] The naval base had been growing, almost by stealth, since the Second World War. At first, an officer was attached incognito to the Bahrain Petroleum Company (BAPCO) in 1946, and the next year the commander-in-chief of Middle East forces began visiting Gulf ports in his flagship. Not long afterwards, the amir complained of the large number of US naval personnel in Bahrain (twenty-four), and by 1956 the commander-in-chief himself was living there, along with the permanent presence of two destroyers of the Sixth Fleet.

THE OIL-PRODUCTION CUTS

On 17 October, Kuwait called a meeting of Arab oil producers, including all Gulf states except Oman. They agreed to cut oil production, using September 1973 level as the starting point. The next day, Saudi Arabia announced its decision to reduce oil production by 10 per cent. On 19 October, in total disregard of the threat to Western economic interests, Nixon asked Congress for $2.2 billion in military assistance to Israel. He was in a particularly tight spot after Spiro Agnew's resignation had placed him in a domestically precarious position. His political reputation was further battered by the enforced resignation of his attorney general and deputy attorney general, and the beginnings of the unravelling of the Watergate scandal. Some analysts have claimed that he deliberately used his support of Israel in Congress to obtain a reprieve from members who wanted his impeachment.[40]

Two days after Nixon's request for the $2.2 billion, Saudi Arabia made a further announcement: that in view of the increased US military support to

Israel, Saudi Arabia had decided to halt the export of oil to the US. Kuwait announced the reduction of oil exports by 10 per cent and a complete stoppage of exports to the USA the same day.

The US ambassador to Saudi Arabia reported that Faisal had unquestionably taken the decision on his own. The diplomat had been with senior Saudi statesmen the day before the announcement, and there had been no hint whatsoever from them. The king was reportedly furious at the $2.2 billion assistance for Israel, and particularly incensed at the difference between the reassuring messages sent to him by the US government and the aid given to Israel. The 'causative effect of pure emotion' should not be overstressed in understanding the king's decision to cut back on oil production.[41]

Faisal and his ministers were determined to pursue the oil cuts—and to increase them, if necessary. They were apparently even prepared for a return to war in the very short term if the oil weapon proved ineffective. Their main strategy was to isolate the European countries and to rely on them to change US policy. The Saudi foreign minister told the British embassy in November that there were three requirements for 'complete friendship' with Saudi Arabia: condemnation of Israeli aggression; recognition of UN Resolution 242; and agreement regarding Palestinian rights to self-determination. The embassy thought it more likely that, despite these stated requirements, the real objective was to alter the US position on the dispute.[42]

The king would have been incensed had he known that Kissinger had already given the 'green light' to the Israeli government to break the ceasefire and overtake Egyptian military positions on the Suez Canal front. This occurred when he met Golda Meir, the Israeli prime minister, in Israel on the very day the ceasefire had been agreed to. Israeli forces broke the ceasefire, surrounding and trapping Egyptian troops, who thereby lost their earlier advantages. Kissinger's go-ahead to Meir was as follows: 'You won't get violent protests from Washington if something happens during the night, while I'm flying. Nothing can happen in Washington until noon tomorrow.'[43]

The recently declassified US National Security Archives disclose various Kissinger policies and stands during and after the conflagration. It is clear that he saw in the war an opportunity to remove the USSR as a major player in the Middle East, and to position the USA as prime mover. This he summed up to Golda Meir when he met her on 22 October as follows: 'My strategy in this crisis ... was to keep the Arabs down and the Russians down.'[44] He was only partially successful in 'keeping the Russians down'.[45] It was not until the Madrid Middle East Conference in 1992 that the USA fully achieved this objective, and then primarily as a result of the collapse of the USSR.

Second, he acted on his own with senior Israelis, in unminuted and undocumented one-to-one meetings with the Israeli ambassador and Golda Meir, the contents of which shall always remain unknown. The documents include such statements as: 'The Prime Minister [Golda Meir] and Dr Kissinger conferred alone for about 15 minutes after Dr Kissinger's arrival.'[46] In the morning meeting referred to above with Dinitz on 9 October 1973, Kissinger also spoke alone with the ambassador for five minutes; and for ten minutes during the evening meeting the same day. There must have been others.

Kissinger was well aware of the weakness of Nixon's position as a result of the many crises facing his administration. He took advantage of the insecurity of Nixon's domestic standing to push forward his own Middle East policy. This came to light when Nixon sent him a message through Brent Scowcroft.[47] The president was exceptionally eager to solve the problem once and for all: 'I now consider a permanent Middle East settlement to be the most important final goal to which we must devote ourselves.' He recognised that failure to do so had been the greatest foreign policy weakness of his administration, and acknowledged that he could deliver his commitments without congressional approval. He instructed Kissinger to proceed by engaging the USSR: both the USA and the USSR had very difficult 'clients', and had to work together to get them in line.

Kissinger was furious when he received these instructions, which went against his objective of marginalising the USSR. He was shocked at what he considered to be the poor judgement of the approach to Brezhnev, and found the instructions to be unacceptable. He chose to ignore them, fully aware of the president's precarious situation and his inability to react to the flouting of his orders.[48]

On 25 October, the USA ordered a military alert because of a perceived nuclear threat from the USSR. Two million US soldiers around the world were mobilised, and information currently being made available indicates more: that the USA was seriously contemplating an invasion of the oilfields of Saudi Arabia, together with Kuwait and the United Arab Emirates, all with vast oil reserves, which had persisted in their embargo of the USA.

According to recently declassified documents, British intelligence claimed in 1973 that the US government was seriously considering such an invasion. James Schlesinger, US defence secretary, apparently informed the British embassy that the USA would not tolerate threats from 'under-developed, under-populated' countries, and that it was no longer obvious to him that the USA could not use force.[49] Although there were only hints at the time that some form of retaliation against the embargo was possible, no further information was given. At a news conference in late November 1973, Kissinger stated that the USA would have to consider counter-measures if the economic pressures continued. He had apparently ordered a number of studies on counter-measures against Arab OPEC members.

British reactions to the threat of an oil embargo were registered basically in one fashion: lie low and hope to be as pro-Arab as possible without being compromised. The records demonstrate that Britain's fundamental attitude was to foster a good relationship with the Arab world. It was generally recognised in the Foreign Office, for example, no British–Arab economic interdependence could succeed without a positive stance regarding the Palestine conflict.

In a telling minute written two months before the war started, David Gore-Booth recommended that Britain should be as overtly pro-Arab as possible, given the UK's commitment to the existence of Israel and the limitations imposed by the British Jewish lobby. This would mean first giving the Arabs all possible political support in the UN, helping the poorer countries, and selling arms.[50] Thus, for example, Douglas-Home stated that Britain would never tolerate the destruction of Israel, all the while instructing his representatives in the Arab world to maintain as close and as pro-Arab a stance as possible.

Faisal's conviction regarding Palestine was strong and determined. The sultan of Oman claimed that the king had become so determined about Palestine that he was talking about the Arabs 'going back to their palm-trees and goats and sand'.[51] Shaikh Khalifah of Qatar regarded him as the toughest of Arab leaders because he had the outlook of an elderly man of religion rather than someone who was primarily motivated by the plight of the Palestinians.[52]

But he was checkmated by his fears: communism, radicalism, revolutionaries. They set a limit to his Arab policies and neutralised his outlook on the Palestine issue. They became overriding concerns as he grew older, a reflection of how much he had changed since 1957 when he told Eisenhower that the Arabs did not share the USA's fear of communism: they had much greater qualms about Israel, which had usurped Arab land. The rise of republicanism, radicalism and socialism in the Arab world, which he regarded as his enemies, had brought about these new suspicions. It is telling that he secretly sanctioned the breaking of the embargo by ARAMCO during late 1973; the embargo had affected the supply of the US navy for the conduct of the Vietnam war. When the US government explained to the king that it required the oil to fight communism, he allowed the supplies to be sent.

His father before him had been hampered by his acknowledgement of the value of his alliance with Britain and the perception of his limited power in the face of British opposition. This was to become a theme with different variations in Saudi history. Faisal had greater limitations. His close relations with the USA were governed by the weaknesses of his strong need for its friendship: not only for its markets, its institutions and its technology, but also for the security it provided his kingdom.

Reactions to the embargo differed in the other Gulf states. In Kuwait, for example, the US ambassador applied for a visit there by Joseph Sisco, a senior State Department official. The Kuwaiti government made it clear that he would not be welcome, an uncharacteristic response which provides a useful gauge of the extent of anti-American feelings there.

Abu Dhabi was opposed to the indiscriminate use of oil as a weapon and wanted to support its friends, such as Britain. But Shaikh Zayid informed the British ambassador that he could not break ranks, and wanted to abide by all decisions to maintain Arab solidarity. He had apparently called the amir of Qatar to suggest a 25 per cent tax on all Arab oil revenues, to be utilised to buy arms to fight Israel. Shaikh Khalifah obviously did not approve. He was worried about the loss of revenue caused by the embargo, especially the losses to his exceptionally large family, many members of whom received substantial sums of money. He was also concerned about the financial losses to Qatar, aware that it did not have the resources of Saudi Arabia: the embargo, combined with heavy financial aid to the war effort, had hit his country, and family.[53] In December, he withdrew Ali Jaidah, Qatar's representative at the talks in Kuwait, from Riyadh talks on participation because he had not followed his brief.[54]

REACTIONS IN EUROPE

The oil embargo caused most Western European countries to alter the course of their overtly pro-Israeli policies. It was perhaps the most palpable and immediate result of the embargo, particularly in the light of US commitments to Israel. One of the objectives of the Saudi strategy was to isolate the European countries and rely on them to alter US policy. In this, it was only partially successful and only in an indirect manner: the Europeans were only able to influence the USA on minor points, not the central issue of resolving the conflict itself.

One week after the war started, the nine members of the EC issued a joint communiqué, calling for a halt to hostilities and negotiations towards a settlement along the lines of UN resolution 242. Not all of them had wanted to go ahead with this statement: Holland and Denmark were against it. But the fears of oil sanctions were so strong that the majority prevailed. A few days later, the EC parliament passed a resolution for the nine governments to help bring about a ceasefire followed by negotiations.[55]

When the Saudi deputy minister for foreign affairs in Jiddah met the representatives of Belgium, France, Germany, Italy, Holland and Britain on 16 October, he thanked them for the gestures, but made it clear they would not be sufficient. This marked the beginning of a new phase for Europe and its relations with the Arab world. It now became less overtly hostile and strove to demonstrate its understanding of the Palestine problem. This contrasted strongly with past patterns: France and Britain had been protagonists in the 1956 Suez war against Egypt; and Britain had supported Israel in the 1967 war.

There was disarray throughout Europe as each country adapted to the new OPEC economic strategy. The position into which these countries were thrown caused them to search for a course that allowed them to differ from the USA in a public way. The Saudis had in effect forced them to pressure the Americans. Ultimately, however, they were unable to influence either the USA or the course of the war; but they were able to provide some political advantages to the Arabs once hostilities were over.

The embargo also impacted on the relations between Europe and the USA, causing a split which lasted for several years. We have already seen how the British Foreign Office, with Douglas-Home at its head, reacted. At first there was conflict between the people and their governments; Gore-Booth referred to the parameters set by the Jewish lobby in the USA and working within them. The war clarified the negative aspects of the 'special relationship' with the USA, a relationship that has been described by more acid observers as a British mindset.

Holland took a pro-Israeli stand from the beginning. Alone in Europe, it allowed NATO bases to be used during the US airlift to Israel. As a result, the oil embargo was extended to the Netherlands. Saudi Arabia was specifically angry with the Netherlands because it was so clearly aiding Israel. When the Dutch ambassador to Iran visited Saudi Arabia, the king refused to see him. The Saudi ambassador to the Netherlands told the government there that pro-Israel remarks by cabinet ministers should be officially repudiated as not being government policy.

After the Arab oil ministers met in Vienna on 18 November, they decided to exclude the nine EC countries from the 5 per cent oil reduction scheduled to begin on 1 December, in appreciation of the political stand they had taken regarding the crisis.[56] The Arab summit of Algiers, held the following week, confirmed the continuation of the cutback and embargo,[57] but excluded Japan and the Philippines because of their pro-Arab declarations. The whole system of embargo and cutbacks was designed to provide favoured nations with just enough oil for their needs, thereby making it difficult for them to send it to other countries; and it was flexible, reversible at any time and to any degree according to the changes in policy of a nation.

Thus, although Europe moved away from its overtly pro-Zionist stance to one that was palpably more accommodating to the Arabs, the USA was unmoved. Its great power and resources allowed it to continue along the same course. The embargo was finally called off in March 1974. Kissinger had convinced Faisal that the USA could not initiate a peace process while it was being embargoed.[58]

There were a number of positive results, mostly initiated by Europe, with the USA in some cases going along with them. Most were related to the position of the PLO and Palestinians in the UN. These will be dealt with in the next chapter.

The most spectacular results, however, were inadvertent. The oil embargo, short-lived though it was, gave the oil-producing countries a new and unforeseen economic boost that converted their economies almost overnight into undreamed-of levels. When the six Gulf members of OPEC (including Iran) met in Kuwait on 16 October 1973, they decided to raise the price of crude oil by 70 per cent. When they met again two months later, they announced another increase, to begin in January 1974: the new price was to be four times as high as it had been on 15 October 1973.[59]

This sudden and totally unexpected jump in prices overwhelmed the Gulf states. Although they had already enjoyed unparalleled prosperity, particularly when compared with their incomes one or two decades earlier, this sudden level of wealth was beyond expectations. The change was felt more acutely by those states that had been so poor only recently. Overnight, within the space of less than three months, their national incomes had quadrupled. The earlier fears of Shaikh Khalifah of Qatar that the embargo would be detrimental to Qatar proved to have been without foundation.

Suddenly, the Gulf states became the focus of an ever-growing number of international companies and entrepreneurs eager to sell products and services to their bemused and bewildered societies. Vast construction and development projects were started, considerable incomes were being generated by these companies and entrepreneurs, and huge profits were accruing, transforming them into modern eldorados. Great fortunes were made by countless persons during those heady days. Many Palestinians lived in the Gulf states: the incomes of the middle-level clerks, teachers, civil servants and others grew accordingly; and the wealthy contractors became very rich indeed.

A new and more impressive link between the Gulf and Palestine was being forged. As the fortunes of the Palestinians living and working in the Gulf grew, they sent considerable remittances to their families, friends and fellow townsmen at home. This money went towards the support of Palestinian individuals and institutions, schools, hospitals, colleges, universities etc. in Palestine, Jordan, Lebanon, Syria and elsewhere. The bounty of the Gulf reached the Palestinians whether at home or in the Diaspora.

There were other links between the two which began to grow at this time. One was the large-scale financial aid from the rulers and governments of the Gulf states to the PLO. The PLO had evolved from being a low-income organisation into a large, well-established quasi-government. It is difficult to estimate the extent of this vast financial support, but there have been a few figures cited. They range from several hundred million to a billion. Few public statements were made about this, but in February 1974, for example, when Arafat was on an official visit to Qatar, the amir pledged full financial support for the information and public relations activities of the PLO. It was then known that Egypt was the main recipient of Qatar's wealth.[60]

The oil money transformed the PLO, as well as the myriad of organisations that sprung up alongside it. The Arab Bank, for example, grew enormously during this period as much of the PLO money was deposited there. The strength of the Arab Bank, loyally supported by most Palestinians, ultimately reflected on the shareholders, whose stocks also grew. This knock-on effect meant that for the first time in decades, many Palestinians were no longer poor.

Other contributions to the PLO exceeded the purely financial. In Kuwait, for example, the government was a strong supporter of the organisation. Its office was upgraded to the status of an embassy, and the PLO representative was regarded as an ambassador, with all the attendant courtesies and benefits. The government was also keen to make its backing of the organisation as public as possible. The Islamic congress in Lahore in early 1974 provided Kuwait with the opportunity to put its weight behind the PLO, politically and diplomatically. The amir of Kuwait took Yasser Arafat on board his flight to Lahore, and insisted on having Arafat beside him at the arrival ceremony at the airport, to be greeted and acknowledged as representative of the Palestinian people and head of the PLO.[61]

Bahrain was more reticent about its links to the PLO. Although the government announced the sanctioning of a PLO office in the country, this did not materialise. Instead, the PLO representative in Qatar acted in Bahrain as well.

The Gulf states continued to spend part of their new and unexpected bounty on the PLO as well as on the 'confrontation' states of Syria, Egypt and Jordan. They bolstered their economies, helped to make good the damage caused by the war, and contributed to strengthening their respective armed forces. The linkage was robust and thriving.

6   The 1980s
Decade of Change

The year 1979 marked a turning point in the modern history of the Middle East, especially the Gulf region. Seven events, whose repercussions were felt throughout the area for many years to come, occurred during that year. Each was highly significant in itself; but their overall effect was seismic in nature, and induced changes which were to alter the region entirely and irrevocably.

No understanding of the Middle East during the early years of the twenty-first century is possible without an awareness of the seeds that were sown during that momentous year. This ultimately impacted on Palestine–Gulf linkage in more ways than one, some more subtly and some more obviously. The full extent of their repercussions was cumulative, and can be readily assessed with hindsight.

The first occurred in January 1979 when Reza Pahlavi, the shah of Iran, was overthrown and fled the country. The triumphant establishment of the Islamic Republic under its leader, Ayatollah Rouhallah Khomeini, ushered in a new era and added a significant dimension to the many changes that swept over the Gulf and the wider region during the coming years. On the international level, the fall of the shah removed the USA's strongest support in the Gulf at one stroke; in fact, the republican government was strongly anti-American. The only part of the twin-pillar policy still intact, the US–Saudi connection, was strengthened by default. And the outbreak of the Iraq–Iran war the next year posed a threat of enormous proportions to the security of the entire region.

The second event was the signing of the Egyptian–Israeli peace agreement on the lawn of the White House in March. President Anwar Sadat of Egypt had expressed his willingness to make a separate peace treaty with Israel even before the 1973 war had started. The National Security Archive reveals the extent to which his envoys embarked on this process during the months preceding the war; the Archive also reveals Kissinger's strategic objective regarding a separate peace treaty between Egypt and Israel, and how this was reflected in his conduct during the 1973 war. Sadat went public with his plans in 1977 after the implementation of Kissinger's policy of step-by-step diplomacy. The bilateral negotiations for the agreement were brokered by the US government.

The foundations of Arab unity, which had been so dramatically displayed during the oil embargo, began to erode. The Arab world fell into disarray—Egypt was ostracised, diplomatic ties were severed and the country was divested of its membership in many Arab regional organisations, starting with the Arab League. Its headquarters, which had always been in Cairo, were moved to Tunis. Two Arab countries, however, refused to disrupt their relationship with Egypt: Morocco and Oman, a Gulf state.

The peace agreement removed Saudi Arabia's only rival for leadership of the Arab world and left it the undisputed leader, strengthened by virtue of its impressive financial power. In early 1975, the elderly and ascetic King Faisal was murdered by his nephew, for reasons never entirely explained. He was succeeded by his brother, King Khalid ibn Abdel Aziz (r. 1975–82), who was an invalid for much of his reign. The most important decision maker in the country during that time was his brother Fahd, the crown prince, a much more worldly figure than Faisal. When Khalid died in 1982, he was succeeded by King Fahd (r. 1982–2005).

The third event occurred in July 1979, when Saddam Hussein ousted Ahmad Hasan Bakr as president of Iraq. He liquidated many of his colleagues and relatives, purging opposition to his rule in a dramatic public meeting which was taped for posterity. As dictator of Iraq, he proceeded to take the inexorable steps towards its decline. In 1979, however, Iraq was still a powerful state with a large standing army. It was not until the following year that his army invaded Iran: the war that followed lasted eight years, devastating both countries and relegating the Palestine problem to second place in the region, leading ultimately to the intifada.

The Baath government, which had come to power in 1968, had shown an interest in the Gulf in a more assertive manner than had previous governments. In the days immediately following the coup that brought it to power, the new Iraqi government had made representations to Britain, then still the colonial power, concerning the Gulf states. It invited Shaikh Zayid of Abu Dhabi on a state visit the same year, and the following year sent its ministers of defence and foreign affairs to the Gulf on official tours. After Britain's 1971 withdrawal, Iraq became a much more forceful presence in the Gulf: although the small states there were very wealthy because of their large oil deposits, they lacked the human resources to overcome the many deficiencies of their social and economic institutions. Iraq stepped in as a neighbour and a fellow Gulf state with an overriding quest for supremacy in the Gulf.

The fourth event took place in Saudi Arabia, one of two upheavals that threatened to undermine its very security that year. This was the seizure of the Grand Mosque at Mecca by a group under the leadership of Juhayman bin Sayf al-Utaybi, a member of the large and powerful Utayba tribe. He and his numerous followers were driven by the deep-rooted desire to restore the purity and essence of Islam to Saudi Arabia. Their motive in seizing its holiest shrine by force of arms was to call attention to what they considered to be the religious laxity prevalent in the kingdom. They regarded the Saudi royal family as having failed in their duty as custodians of the Grand Mosque to maintain the original mission of the Wahhabi movement. The Saudi government was finally able to dislodge the rebels, but not before scores were injured and many killed. The siege ended when its leaders finally ran out of ammunition and surrendered. It has been said that a French anti-terrorist squad planned the final assault, which was carried out by the Saudi National Guard.

The fifth event erupted in the rich, oil-producing province of Hasa, on the eastern coast of Saudi Arabia. Its population is mainly Shia, and as such was regarded as the Achilles heel of Saudi Arabia, particularly since the establishment of the Islamic Republic in Iran. It had long been governed by different members of the Ibn Jiluwi family, related to the Al Saud, who were renowned for the close control they exercised over the province. This control was deeply resented by the Hasawis (people of Hasa), who were also bitter about having received very little of the enormous wealth of the country compared with their compatriots elsewhere, although they constituted the backbone of the labour force in the oilfields that produced that wealth.

Encouraged by the militant Shiism of the Iranian Republic as well as by the siege of the Grand Mosque, which was just coming to an end, the leaders of the Shia community announced they would be marching in public during Ashura (the commemoration of the deaths of the Prophet's grandsons Hasan and Husain), in open defiance of a long-standing law banning any demonstrations on that day. When a policeman struck a demonstrator, there was almost immediate reaction. Crowds thronged the streets in the city of Qatif, setting fire to cars, breaking into shops and looting. Seventeen people were killed and many wounded.

Both rebellions shook the Saudi government. The Grand Mosque episode had threatened its essential role as custodian of the holiest shrine of Islam and questioned the legitimacy of the Al Saud. The Shia riots underlined the vulnerability of the oil-producing province and raised the possibility that its people, who had so many resentments against Saudi rule, might turn to Iran for guidance and leadership. In an attempt to heal the breach with the Hasawis, the government earmarked large sums of money to improve housing, health and education. Ibn Jaluwi was removed as governor and replaced by Prince Muhammad bin Fahd (son of the crown prince), who immediately set about trying to improve relations.

Saudi Arabia turned more openly than ever before to the USA for military support to withstand the forces, both external and internal, that it found difficult to contain. There were other repercussions. The king was now referred to as the Custodian of the Holy Places, a reinforcement of the role of the royal family as the guardians of Wahhabism. He authorised the setting up of a consultative council (*majlis al-shura*), the first formal attempt at broadening political participation, but it was not actually decreed until 1992, after the cataclysmic events following the Iraqi invasion of Kuwait. It is interesting to note here that the concept of a *majlis al-shura* had first been aired in 1948 after the equally devastating events surrounding the creation of Israel: the disquiet of the people was then reflected in graffiti on the walls of the Great Mosque in Mecca, and King Abdel Aziz responded by raising the possibility of establishing such a *majlis*.

Other measures to counteract the accusations of Juhayman were swiftly implemented. These concerned a tightening of Islamic laws and principles. The school curriculum was drastically amended to focus more deeply on such subjects as Islamic law and jurisprudence, Islamic ideals etc. This narrowing of the education system was a contributing factor to the high levels of unemployment in the country which is causing such disquiet amongst the youth today: they are ill-equipped to join the labour force of the twenty-first century, immersed as they are in subjects whose practical applications are very limited.

The sixth event catapulted the USA into the region when fifty-two American hostages were seized in Iran in retaliation for the exiled shah's arrival in the USA. The hostage crisis marked a new departure for the USA: a foreign policy issue in the Middle East was transformed into a subject of great domestic concern. The fate of the prisoners became of such vital importance that it contributed to Jimmy Carter's loss of the presidency at the next election. Iran and the Persian Gulf were no longer remote areas to the American people: they had become of central interest as the fate of the hostages was aired daily on the media.

The seventh event occurred during the final days of the year, when the Soviet army invaded Afghanistan. The 1980s therefore started on the heels of these seven milestones. The new focus of US policy in the region was to become the first step to the full-scale presence of US forces in the Gulf by the end of the century. The role of Saudi Arabia as a US ally in the final phases of the Cold War became of paramount importance. Palestine receded into second place in international affairs after having occupied centre stage since 1973.

FIGHTING THE 'EVIL EMPIRE'

The start of Fahd's reign coincided with the strengthening and expansion of Saudi Arabia's strategic alliance with the USA, which was to alter the triangular relationship in more ways than one. Their common overriding fears of an entrenched Shia opposition after the Ashura riots, coupled with the rising powers of republican Iran, brought the two closer than ever before. The Soviet occupation of Afghanistan strengthened the alliance, as both viewed this added threat to Sunni Islam with alarm. The US–Saudi partnership grew in pursuit of their common objectives. The USA wanted to roll back Soviet expansionism, not only in Afghanistan, but in places such as Nicaragua; Saudi Arabia viewed the Soviet occupation of Afghanistan as a direct threat, and at the same time wanted to curtail growing Shia power in the Gulf by underlining its own strong Sunni foundations. The new US policy came into being almost immediately after the inauguration of Ronald Reagan as president in January 1980.

The Reagan doctrine, as it became known, marked a departure in US policy regarding the Cold War. Whereas post-war policy had focused on containment of the USSR, it now became much more aggressive, devoted as it was to reversing Soviet expansionism. The concept of the Evil Empire was born, and with it the covert support of anti-insurgent movements against the USSR in the Third World: this included the Contras, as the anti-Sandinistas were known, in Nicaragua; and the Mujahideen movement in Afghanistan. It has been estimated that the Mujahideen alone received $3 billion from the US and Saudi Arabia combined, and that the Contras got $32 million from Saudi Arabia. Both proxy armies received US training, plus economic and political support. Saudi Arabia supported the Mujahideen by providing them with arms and money, much as it had covertly supplied financial aid to combat Soviet influence in Angola and Mozambique. The US–Saudi policy during this time has been described by Rachel Bronson, of the New York Council of Foreign Relations, as a partnership that went beyond being a financial relationship. They were ideologically compatible, united in their attitude towards communism and godlessness: the USA attacked communism, Saudi Arabia sought to end godlessness.[1]

The Saudi portion of the twin-pillar policy of the USA was deepened throughout the 1980s.

LINKS WITH PALESTINE

Arab linkage continued during the 1980s. A number of examples can be cited during the following years. Some were on the national and international levels, others on the circumstantial and personal. One example of the latter was the murder in 1977 of Dr Sayf bin Ghubash, the UAE's minister of state for foreign affairs, a brilliant and rising star of the new country. He was bidding farewell at Abu Dhabi airport to the Syrian foreign minister, who had just ended a visit to the country, when a young Palestinian, enraged at Syria's role in the battles in the Palestinian refugee camp of Tal al-Zaatar, north of Beirut, tried to kill the Syrian official; he missed and hit Ghubash, who died almost immediately.

The year 1979 contained an instance of linkage which, although very much on the personal level, somehow transcended it to become almost institutional. It fitted neatly into the old triangular pattern between the USA, Palestine and the Gulf. Andrew Young, a distinguished American statesman, had been a Georgia congressman for three terms, and was appointed US ambassador to the UN during the administration of his fellow Georgian, Jimmy Carter. In keeping with US policy, he had refused all contact with the PLO and its representatives, which his government regarded as terrorists.

But he agreed to become part of what must have been a trial balloon when he went along with his five-year-old son to visit Abdullah Yacoub Bishara, the Kuwaiti ambassador to the UN, who also had a young son. He knew that Labib Terzi, the PLO spokesman at the UN, would be there. Young wanted to see him, aware that the UN Committee of Palestinian Rights was about to put forward a resolution to the Security Council which, with hindsight, contained many of the elements that were later to be incorporated in the 1993 Oslo Agreement. Although the USA had been trying for years to influence the PLO to recognise Israel, Young considered that the timing was not right for the Carter administration. As president of the Security Council, he wanted to meet informally and off the record to ask the PLO to postpone the resolution. The Arab ambassadors were meeting at the home of Bishara, and wanted Young to put his request straight to Terzi.

The meeting had been cleared by the State Department, and it was agreed that the US government would say that it was a chance meeting and no official business was discussed. Young also gave the Israeli ambassador a full report, which was later passed on to the foreign minister (Moshe Dayan).

Fourteen years later, in an interview, Young claimed that he had had to resign because of the headlines of the tabloid newspapers in New York: that of the *New York Post*, for example, was 'Jews demand firing Young'. He finally resigned in September 1979, despite having had a 100 per cent pro-Israel voting record in Congress.[2]

THE VENICE DECLARATION

The situation in Iran caused great turmoil in the financial markets of the West. The instability was largely linked to the uncertainties of oil production: during the first seven months after the revolution, there was a decline of between 2 and 2.5 million barrels a day. During the first year after the Iraqi invasion of Iran and the ensuing war, the combined production of the two countries dropped by 6.5 million barrels a day. As a result, the price of oil more than doubled from 1978 to 1981. Europe was the most severely affected as the international oil markets panicked.

Europe, of course, had traditional ties and common interests with the Middle East, and, in a bid to win favour amongst Arab countries, the nine members of the EC made a political statement regarding the issue of Palestine. With the situation in Palestine deteriorating rapidly and no sign of Israeli withdrawal from occupied territories, the EC issued what became known as the Venice Declaration after meeting there in June 1980. It reaffirmed support for UN resolutions 242 and 338 and committed itself to the rights of all states, including Israel, to exist in security in the Middle East; and to justice for all peoples in the region, recognising the legitimate rights of the Palestinians. There can be little doubt that the Venice Declaration was directly linked to the oil markets of the Gulf.

The US reaction to the 1979 events in the Gulf, including the fall of the shah, the creation of the Islamic Republic and the seizure of American hostages, was of a geo-strategic nature. It enunciated its new policy in what became known as the Carter doctrine. In his January 1980 State of the Union speech, President Carter referred in no uncertain terms to the US position in the Gulf: he made it clear that any attempt by outside forces to gain control of the region would be regarded as an assault on the vital interests of the USA, and that America would repel such an assault.

The Iraqi invasion of Iran in September 1980 put paid to further serious European statements. The two titans of the Gulf were now locked in battles of gigantic proportions, and the problems of Palestine faded into the background. The Iraq-Iran war lasted for eight years, way beyond the original expectations of the invading Iraqis. It left a trail of destruction in its wake. An estimated one million people died, many were wounded, and huge numbers were taken prisoner. The fighting went through many phases, as both sides gained and lost. At the start of the war, Iraq was firmly in the Soviet orbit, relying heavily on the USSR for its military equipment. It had severed ties with the USA after the June 1967 Arab–Israeli war because of the close US–Israeli alliance.

After 1984, Iraq and the USA renewed their diplomatic relations, and within three years Iraq had become America's third-largest trading partner in the Middle East. The new Iraqi relationship with the USA was kept largely secret: many aspects of the enormous aid provided by America in the conduct of the war were only revealed much later. Likewise, Iran's earlier antagonism to the USSR changed when, in 1987, the two signed a treaty of friendship and cooperation, including collaboration in a number of fields.

THE FORMATION OF THE GCC

In February 1981, a few months after the outbreak of the Iraq–Iran war, the foreign ministers of the five Gulf states and Saudi Arabia held a meeting in Riyadh. They had come together in direct response to the new challenges threatening the region, and to seek a collective course of action. Before the end of the meeting, they had decided to form a regional political grouping, the Gulf Cooperation Council (GCC). Its official inauguration took place in May 1981 when the six heads of state met in Abu Dhabi. Security was the main stimulus of the new organisation, but its declared objective was to effect the social and economic integration of the member states.

The GCC was created to counter the threats to the Arab states of the region from Iran and the USSR. As these threats receded and new ones emerged, the Council has strengthened many institutions of the member states. It has done away with many social and economic restrictions on its nationals, it has introduced a customs union, and over the years has solidified its external policies. But when it was created, security in its immediate vicinity was its main focus.

In June 1981, the Israeli air force flew over Jordan and Saudi Arabia to bomb the Osirak nuclear reactor in Baghdad. This brought the problem of Palestine practically to the shores of the Gulf for the first time since British withdrawal ten years earlier. In early August that year, the USA had entered into secret talks with the PLO regarding a possible peace treaty with Israel.

That same month, Crown Prince Fahd of Saudi Arabia presented his eight-point peace plan, which marked a departure for a core Arab state: for the first time, it acknowledged that all states in the region, obviously including Israel, should live in peace (point 7). Other points were that Israel would withdraw from territories it had occupied in 1967; that Israeli settlements would be dismantled; that Palestinians had the right of return; and that an independent Palestinian state would be set up.

Exactly two months later, Anwar Sadat was assassinated, and by the end of the year Israel had extended its rule to the Golan, effectively annexing the area. Fahd's peace plan had little chance of survival, particularly when in June 1982, Israeli forces invaded Lebanon, where they were to remain for several months, attacking the PLO headquarters, and wounding and killing thousands of civilians. By the end of the summer, the PLO was forced to leave Lebanon and settle in Tunis, also the headquarters of the Arab League.

A new peace plan was proposed in September 1982, this time by Ronald Reagan, US president since January 1981. It called for Palestinian self-government in association with Jordan, firmly refusing the idea of an independent state. It also refused to sanction Israeli annexation or permanent control of the West Bank and Gaza in accordance with UN Resolution 242.

In response to the Reagan plan, the Arab League summit made what became known as the Fez Declaration of September 1982. Consisting of eight points, it reiterated many of the ideas contained in the Fahd plan; this included peace between all states of the region, including a Palestinian state, to be guaranteed by the Security Council.

THE AWACS AND US POLICY, 1981

In 1981, the links between the Gulf and Palestine were underlined again, this time in the case of Saudi arms purchases. In May 1978, the US administration had pledged limitations on future arms sales to Saudi Arabia in order to obtain Senate approval of the sale of F-15 aircraft to Saudi Arabia. In a letter to the chairman of the Senate Foreign Relations Committee, the secretary of defence stated that the F-15s would not be equipped with special features that would give them additional range and that they would not have the equipment that would allow the planes to carry a substantial bomb load.[3]

After the fall of the shah and the invasion of Afghanistan, however, Saudi Arabia sought better protection from the growing air threat to its security. It requested additional equipment for its aircraft, to extend their range and capabilities. This provoked a major US–Saudi crisis. Sixty-eight senators, more than two-thirds of the Senate, signed a letter to President Carter objecting to such a sale.[4] Their objection was based on fears that such equipment could be utilised to attack Israel. Carter had no choice in the matter, especially during an election year, but told the Saudi government quietly to reapply for the equipment once elections were over. In a clear pre-election statement, however, Carter stated: 'We will not agree to provide offensive capabilities for the planes that might be used against Israel.'[5]

Carter lost the election, and Reagan became president. The Saudi government then tied the issue of US military sales to US requests for financial aid to the Mujahideen, the militant Islamic group who were fighting the Soviet occupation of Afghanistan. The USA wanted Saudi Arabia to increase the financial aid it was giving the fighters; but the Saudi government refused to do so until America sanctioned the purchase of military equipment. The Saudi Third Five-Year Plan, issued in May 1980, had emphasised an expansion of military equipment and infrastructure to meet the new requirements of the political environment. It was at this point that the new Reagan administration put together what became known as the Saudi Air Defence Enhancement Package.

Less than two weeks after Reagan's inauguration, the Saudi minister of information stated in an American TV interview that the Camp David agreements had not brought about a comprehensive peace, and that the rights of the Palestinians had yet to be addressed. This interview placed Saudi Arabia once again firmly on the map of the Palestine problem. Linkage was clear for all to see. A former US ambassador to Saudi Arabia, James Akins, expressed the innate Arabism of the Saudis and quoted King Faisal's famous statement that communism was the mother of Zionism. He admitted that such a formula was not often heard in the Middle East after Faisal's death, but added that there was a widespread belief throughout the Arab world and beyond that US support of the partition of Palestine and its ongoing support of Israel had opened up the entire region to the USSR.

Akins stated that Faisal had been committed to Arab–American friendship and regarded US policy towards Israel as an aberration. He had a clear vision of where US interests lay and thought that eventually the USA would recognise this, taking a more balanced position in the region.[6]

The Reagan administration announced its new Middle Eastern policy, whose priorities were to bolster the position of the West in the face of Soviet threats. It presented Congress with the basic outline of a proposed arms package for Saudi Arabia: AIM-9L missiles, conformal fuel tanks and five AWACs. This met with fierce opposition in Congress.

Twenty senators immediately announced they were against such a sale, and the opposition soon grew. Saudi arms purchases from the USA were sometimes complicated by 'an increasingly assertive American Jewish community, whose pro-Israel lobby, the American Israel Public Affairs Committee (AIPAC) opposed sales of advanced arms ... on the basis that they might be employed against Israel.'[7]

AIPAC's strategy was to seek congressional votes against the arms purchases; Saudi Arabia, lacking such an option, worked through the administration. As in 1978, when F-15s were delivered, the administration won.

It was not an easy battle, despite the fact that AIPAC regarded its inability to stop the sale as a major failure. Both sides lobbied hard, and the final vote reflected the intensity of both positions. Fifty-two senators were for the sale, forty-eight against. The total cost of the package was $8.5 billion, a not inconsiderable sum in 1981. Moreover, there were significant conditions attached to the sale: the USA retained the right of continual on-site inspection and surveillance by US personnel of security arrangements for all operations; no citizens of third nations would be permitted to maintain or modify equipment; computer software remained the property of the USA; Saudi Arabia would share all information acquired from the equipment. Reagan assured Congress that the transfer of equipment would not take place until he had certified that all the conditions had been met. When Saudi Arabia took possession of the five AWACs in 1986, Reagan confirmed that this had been done in a letter to the Senate majority leader.

The Reagan administration won because of the strength of US foreign policy, which was to defeat the USSR on all fronts in the Cold War. The sale to Saudi Arabia of the AWACs was considered to have been a sharp upturn in the US–Saudi partnership.

It was not, however, an indication of any change in US policy towards Israel. Israel was shaken by its defeat in Congress. One of the outcomes was the strengthening of its lobbying apparatus in the USA. AIPAC intensified its efforts to prevent another such incident, and succeeded in boosting both its membership and its budget dramatically.

A Memorandum of Understanding on Strategic Cooperation between the US and Israeli governments followed later that year (30 November 1981). Joint military exercises between the two countries were agreed on, as well as cooperation in research and development, and in defence trade. In January 1987, Congress designated Israel a major non-NATO ally, and sanctioned it to bid on classified defence contracts. And in April 1988, another Memorandum of Understanding between the USA and Israel was signed; this institutionalised the strategic relationship.

It was not until 1985 that AIPAC was able to secure a victory by temporarily blocking the sale of additional F-15s through Congress. Congress also blocked the sale to Saudi Arabia of short-range surface-to-surface missiles and continued to intervene to block sales of missiles of all kinds. That year, Bandar bin Sultan, Saudi ambassador to the USA, made a secret trip to Beijing to negotiate a multi-billion dollar deal for an estimated ten to fifteen mobile launchers and between fifty and fifty-six specially modified missiles.[8]

The USA made public its displeasure at the sale and the fact that its ally in the fight against communism had bought arms from a communist country. Sarcasm was also used, particularly when a senior member of the government pointed out the irony of the sale, which had made Saudi Arabia vulnerable to Israeli aggression. The assistant secretary for defence apparently congratulated Bandar, telling him about the law of unintended consequences: 'You have put Saudi Arabia squarely in the targeting package of the Israelis. You are now number one on the Israeli hit parade. If the balloon goes up anywhere in the Middle East, you're going to get hit first.'[9]

But Bandar made it clear that this step was taken only as a result of congressional interventions on arms sales. Saudi Arabia wanted to assert its independence from American arms policy. But it did not disassociate itself from the Palestine problem, which involved it in the fiercely anti-Saudi congressional debates and votes. Saudi attempts to obtain US arms continued to face opposition because of the Arab–Israeli conflict, despite the important strategic role it played in US foreign policy during the Reagan era.

In November 1983, Israel signed another agreement with the USA, which created a Joint Political and Military Group.

IRANGATE, 1986

When the so-called 'Irangate' story hit the front pages of the media worldwide, the connection between the US and Iran was reinforced, albeit in a rather obtuse and roundabout manner. In early November 1986, *al-Shira'a* (a Lebanese weekly) revealed that senior US officials had gone on a secret mission to Tehran to make available spare parts and ammunition in exchange for the release of American hostages in Lebanon.

The article started the process of unravelling some of the intricacies of the elaborate Iran–Contra affair. The Reagan administration had secretly sold arms and ammunition to Iran for its war against Iraq, and had then diverted the proceeds of the sales to the rebel Contras in Nicaragua who were fighting to overthrow the Sandinista government.

Both were illicit: trading arms for hostages despite US policy that America would never make concessions to terrorists; and providing paramilitary aid to the Contras in violation of the Congressional ban known as the Noland Amendment (1984). The Reagan administration sent millions of dollars to the Contras from the proceeds of the Iran sales after Congress had cut off funding to the rebel guerrillas.

The USA had thus contravened its own embargo when it sold arms and ammunition to Iran in 1985 and 1986. It did this both directly and indirectly, through Israel. In fact, a joint US–Israeli operation in 1985 provided Iran with arms in exchange for the release of hostages in Lebanon. Moreover, Lieutenant Colonel Oliver North (the National Security Council member in charge of the operation) admitted later that he had had secret talks with Iranian officials during those years and had indicated to them that the USA would be willing to overthrow Saddam Hussein.[10]

Saudi Arabia was also involved in the scandal: it had secretly transferred a total of $32 million to the Contras at the request of US national security adviser, Robert McFarlane. There is no indication, however, that Saudi Arabia had any knowledge of the scope of the operation, nor was it aware of other participants in the conspiracy. These included Israel, China, Taiwan, Panama, Costa Rica, Guatemala, El Salvador and Honduras.

Saudi Arabia's role was limited to the transfer of funds to Nicaragua in support of Reagan's policy of 'rolling back' leftist and communist governments worldwide. Israel's, by contrast, was fundamental to the entire operation as seen in the recently declassified National Security Archive documents. One example of this encapsulates the close arrangements between the two governments: the Pentagon bought Russian arms from Israel, which had captured them from the PLO in Lebanon, and then sent them to the Contras. This was a plan worked on by US and Israeli officials. They also worked together in the arms-for-hostages plan in Iran.[11]

After details of Iran–Contra began to filter out, US efforts to aid Iran by providing armaments came to an end. The help it was providing Iraq, however, continued, and remained largely unknown until several years later.

THE FIRST INTIFADA

Iran–Contra explained some of the mysteries of the conflicting attitudes taken by the USA and other countries towards the Iraq–Iran war. With time and the declassification of further state documents, it has become clear that a prolonged war between the two Gulf powers served the interests of many countries. A US statesman is quoted as having said at the time: 'A pity only one side can lose.' Even Saddam Hussein, a recipient of significant—albeit secret—aid from the USA, accused that country of pursuing a policy to continue the war.

His assessment was obviously accurate. While one branch of the US government had been secretly supplying Iran with arms, another (the CIA) had been providing the Iraqi air force with sensitive satellite pictures of Iranian targets. It appears that aid to Iran stopped after 1986, but continued to Iraq until the end of the war.

The declassified National Security Archive indicates the extent to which the US government was involved in providing covert assistance to Iraq throughout the 1980s. Senior members of the government, including Donald Rumsfeld, as representative of the president, met senior Iraqi politicians, and facilitated the promotion of closer ties between the two countries.

The Commerce Department files disclosed the approval of exports to Iraq for 'military recipients and others involved in military research and development, including the Iraqi Air Force, Iraq's Ministry of Defence, the Saad General Establishment (missile research), the State Organization for Technical Industries (military production) and al-Qaqaa State Establishment (explosives and propellants research and production)'.[12] Despite the use of chemical weapons during the war, the Reagan administration argued against the imposition of sanctions on Iraq. Other exports included dual-use technology with potential civilian uses and military applications, such as ultra-sophisticated computers, armoured ambulances, helicopters and chemicals.

Financial aid was also forthcoming. Iraqi military spending is estimated to have been over $110 billion during the war. The USA secretly provided loans, utilising a foreign bank based in America to effect the transfers. In 1989, the FBI raided the Atlanta (Georgia) branch of the Italian bank Banca Nazionale del Lavoro, whose shares were almost totally owned by the Italian government. The bank had secretly provided massive loans to foreign countries, including Iraq. It was later disclosed that $5 billion had been transferred to Iraq from that branch alone during the period 1985–9. The branch had also handled a large portion of US agricultural credit guarantees for Iraq, and had provided financing for non-agricultural exports. This followed the decision made by Reagan in July 1982 when he secretly committed the USA to do anything necessary to prevent Iraq losing the war.[13]

Both sides spent billions of dollars on arms and ammunition, which were supplied by governments and arms dealers that sold their wares to both adversaries. Countries involved spanned the globe: China, the USSR, the USA, the UK, France, Italy, North Korea, Poland, Romania and Czechoslovakia were some of these.

The war stimulated the other Gulf states to purchase huge amounts of arms in an effort to defend themselves in case of a spillover of the fighting. Since they all had enormous budgets for defence, running into many billions of dollars, arms manufacturers and dealers worldwide once again reaped rich financial rewards.

Iraq also received financial help from its Arab neighbours, particularly those with large oil budgets. Kuwait and Saudi Arabia were the two largest donors: they supplied outright gifts, and they provided loans. By the end of the war, Iraq owed Kuwait $30 billion. The collapse of oil prices, together with unemployment, inflation and foreign debt left Iraq in severe financial straits at the end of the war.

But even before the war was over, and despite the covert aid bestowed by so many Western countries, Iraq faced the possibility of defeat when in

1986 Iranian forces occupied Fao. This loss of an integral part of Iraqi territory increased Arab fears in the Gulf, as Iranian missiles now had reached striking distance of Kuwait. Kuwait had been subjected to an increasing number of acts of sabotage, including fires at an oil complex, a car bomb in downtown Kuwait, and a shell fired at Failaka island.

The summer of 1987 was a particularly hot one in the Gulf; temperatures soared well above normal and the humidity was uncomfortably higher than usual. The focus, however, was not so much on the temperature as on the heat generated by the growing armada of foreign ships in the Gulf, against a background of repeated Iranian threats against interference.

Saudi Arabia had also had its fair share of troubles with Iran. In late July 1987, Mecca became the scene of angry demonstrations by Iranian pilgrims, which resulted in the deaths of several hundred people. This took place during the annual Hajj (pilgrimage), when the city was teeming with pilgrims from all over the world. Although details of the actual events have fluctuated according to source, it is clear that the Iranian pilgrims had assembled near the Grand Mosque and led a demonstration against the policies of the USA, the USSR and Israel. Political demonstrations during the Hajj were banned, so Saudi security forces were called in. According to one version (Iranian), the police opened fire on Iranian pilgrims, and some 600 people were killed and another 2,000 wounded. Another version (Saudi) was that Saudi forces attempted to restrain the Iranian demonstration; they used tear gas, but were otherwise unarmed. The ensuing panic amongst the huge crowds (there were 2,000,000 pilgrims that year) caused many to be trampled to death in the crush; 402 people were killed, of whom a large proportion were Iranian. Two days later, the Saudi and Kuwaiti embassies in Tehran were attacked and occupied.

The Mecca crisis acted as a catalyst in unifying divergent Arab positions. Iraq desperately rallied its fellow Arabs to the rescue, and was supported in this by Kuwait and Saudi Arabia. In November 1987, an Extraordinary Arab Summit was held in Amman. It had been preceded by Jordanian diplomatic efforts. These involved convincing Hafez al-Asad of Syria, the main Arab ally of Iran, to attend; and, having done so, to establish some sort of reconciliation between Syria and Iraq. The continuing feud between these two countries had been a significant impediment to the formation of a united stand against Iran. At the Amman summit, however, Arab leaders appeared to have closed ranks.

The Gulf war was the first and central point of the discussions, as evinced in the final declaration. The heads of state expressed their indignation at Iran's insistence on prolonging the war. They condemned the Islamic Republic for occupying Arab land and for procrastination in accepting Security Council Resolution 598 (July 1987), which called for a ceasefire and a withdrawal of all warring forces. They expressed strong support for Saudi Arabia and Kuwait in the face of Iranian threats. It is very significant that they also sanctioned the resumption of relations with Egypt, allowing Kuwait to accept Egyptian military assistance.[14]

The issue of Palestine was relegated to second place for the first time since the establishment of the Arab League in 1945. The League had itself been set up in direct response to the threat of large-scale foreign immigration into Palestine in the 1940s. The Great Revolt of 1936–9 had been the reason for the creation of the organisation. Practically all summits since then had been devoted to the problems caused by the ever-present conflict as it evolved from phase to phase.

Reference to Palestine at the 1987 Amman summit was limited to vague statements about peace only being possible through the recovery of occupied land and the restoration of the rights of the Palestinians. No new ideas were presented and no new promises made. It was clear that Arab resources, human and financial, were being diverted to the Gulf.

There is little doubt that the beginning of the intifada was linked to this summit meeting. The Palestinian situation had been deteriorating steadily during the years of the Iraq–Iran war. With the attention of the superpowers fixed on the security of the Gulf and the production of oil, one event after another regarding Palestine went onto the back burner. Thus, in December 1981, when Israel extended its rule to the Golan, effectively annexing it, protests from the USA and leading powers were muted and short-lived. The massive Israeli invasion of Lebanon in June 1982 evinced only mild rebukes from the USA, with calls to both sides for moderation.

It was only after widespread international condemnation of the September 1982 massacres at the Palestinian camps of Sabra and Chatila in Beirut that Western governments began to react by sending in token military forces to protect the Palestinian people in Lebanon. This coincided with the announcement of yet another peace plan: this one, the Reagan Peace Plan, limited Palestinian sovereignty to some form of autonomy within Jordan.

In the mean time, the situation of the Palestinians continued to deteriorate, with little signs of a serious breakthrough on any front. In October 1985, Israel mounted a massive bombing raid on PLO headquarters in Tunisia, killing over seventy people and injuring many. In 1986, the government of Jordan closed PLO offices there, and deported Khalil al-Wazir, one of the leaders of Fatah, who was responsible for resistance in the Occupied Territories; the following year the US government closed down the Palestine Information Office in Washington DC. In June 1987, Jewish settlers in Gaza went on a rampage; they attacked two Palestinian truck drivers. The Israeli occupying forces declared the Ballata refugee camp a closed military area; they arrested and deported several people. The residents joined a large protest, which the Israeli forces countered with teargas and rubber bullets. The settlers continued to attack refugees: a few days later, they raided the Dheisheh camp, and vandalised homes there. The following month, Israeli military authorities placed an indefinite ban on fishing in Gaza, effectively cutting off the livelihood of all of the city's fishermen.

In October 1987, a general strike in the West Bank and Gaza was observed in protest against the visit of George Schultz, the US secretary of state. The Palestinians also felt isolated by the growing concerns in the Arab world for the faltering military status of Iraq; Egyptian attendance at a meeting of the Islamic Organisation Conference in January 1987 was regarded as an indication of approaching normalisation with Egypt since it had signed the peace agreement with Egypt. In April, Saddam Hussein and Hafez al-Asad, erstwhile enemies, met to discuss the war in the Gulf, thereby reducing emphasis on the rapidly deteriorating conditions in Palestine.

It was only to be expected, therefore, that when, on 9 December 1987, an Israeli truck collided with a group of Palestinians, killing four, the funerals would become the focus of widespread national fury, heralding the start of the first intifada.

While it cannot be stated that this was directly caused by the situation in the Gulf, the link between the two is undeniable. Once again, international concern for Palestine was connected to affairs in the Gulf. It was not to be until August 1990 that this link was broken.

The end of this linkage constituted a major qualitative difference from other stages within the general connection between Palestine and the Gulf region. Hitherto, events emanating in Palestine had activated links with the Gulf; in this case, however, those whose roots were in different parts of the greater Gulf region had major repercussions on Palestine. They effectively precipitated a new departure for Palestinian development. Furthermore, the seven momentous events of 1979 had had a dramatic impact on the political environments of both the Gulf and Palestine, although perhaps not in an equal or similar fashion.

7 The United Nations
The Triangle without Corners

The 1973 war revealed the strong links between Palestine and the Gulf for the first time, uniting both against continued US support for Israel. It was a new and different position for the Gulf states, and was to become more visible throughout the remainder of the decade. The increasing visibility itself was a new departure; the region moved into centre stage of relations with the West until 1990, when the Iraqi invasion of Kuwait was to alter the situation.

All the Gulf states were now independent and could exercise their own foreign policies, in some cases for the very first time. Furthermore, they were substantial oil exporters and thus had economic power. Oil supplies were abundant but because of the relative importance of all Arab countries in the oil market (including Algeria, Iraq and Libya) they had genuine power to influence the international availability of oil.

Fuel conservation and energy efficiency had become an overwhelming priority in the industrial world. Massive projects to develop alternative sources of energy were initiated. In the mean time, industries that had relied on unlimited supplies of cheap oil became unable to continue production; many had to alter course. Long queues of motorists waiting for petrol became a common sight in Europe and the USA as fuel levels hit transportation. Speed limits were imposed to improve the efficiency of energy use, and drastic measures were taken to cut down on the heating of homes, schools and factories as millions faced the prospect of a cold and dark winter. In the UK, a three-day week was introduced in response to the crisis.

Desperate for oil, governments and major institutions became prepared to pay much higher prices. These rose dramatically from $3 to $17 a barrel. There was a corresponding rise in the cost of living worldwide, and the inevitable inflation was accompanied by widespread economic recession. The quadrupling of oil prices within a few months of the end of the war made the Gulf region one of the most sought after and desirable in the world.

Although the oil embargo did not succeed in inducing a change in US policy towards Israel, it had a number of important repercussions. Most outstanding perhaps is what became known as 'Arab linkage strategy': the integration of government policy in Saudi Arabia and the Gulf states with events in the northern part of the Arab world. This was a new departure, because of the previously limited direct linkage between the two sides. Although Saudi Arabia had utilised what it termed its 'oil weapon' against France and Britain in 1956 and 1967, it had carried little weight because it had acted alone at a time when an oil glut in the international market curtailed the effectiveness of the strategy.

Bahrain, Qatar and the UAE had, of course, been outside the mainstream of the Arab world until 1971 when they became fully independent. British policy had carefully sought to maintain that separateness. Although events leading to the establishment of the 1938 reform movement in Kuwait were connected with the Palestine crisis of 1936–9, this kind of linkage was a phenomenon rather than a common occurrence. Once oil was discovered in the Gulf states, Britain became even more reluctant to allow the states to engage with the northern Arab world.[1]

The oil embargo occurred only two years after Britain had withdrawn its forces from the Gulf. It demonstrated the intrinsic Arab nature of the Gulf states despite 150 years of British attempts to isolate them. Linkage strategy presented the first pan-Arab effort to close ranks against the USA and other countries that persisted in aiding Israel. In 1974, at a meeting of the Arab heads of state in Rabat, the PLO was recognised as the sole legitimate representative of the Palestinian people. The question of Palestine was given institutional backing for the first time; and its centrality in Arab politics was re-emphasised.

Arab linkage strategy was a manifestation of the close integration of the Gulf with the rest of the Arab world. It represented an important step in the process of increased interaction between the two; the most significant contemporary link between them remained the Palestine problem. This grew during the remainder of the 1970s and the 1980s, but went into sharp decline after the Iraqi invasion of Kuwait in 1990.

EUROPE'S NEW ROLE

Europe was just beginning to evince its participation as a possible mediator in the Arab–Israeli dispute. It was careful to distance itself as much as possible from the position of the USA. In this, it saw the UN as a useful international organisation in which to express its support for the Palestinians and thereby hopefully to obtain the financial and economic benefits of friendship with the super-rich states of the Gulf. In this, it was mindful of the role worked out by the Saudi government at the very beginning of the war when it told the European ambassadors that it would use the oil weapon to persuade them to obtain a change in US policy in the Middle East.

The UN had grown substantially during the 1960s and into the 1970s when the former colonies of Africa and Asia won their independence and took their places alongside other sovereign states in the organisation. In

1948, the UN had 51 member states; by 1999, these had become 188.[2] With one vote each in the General Assembly, they could act together to influence the voting. The Security Council, of course, remained the preserve of the Big Five, whose veto power continued to dominate proceedings.

The problem of Palestine had long and historical links with the United Nations and its antecedent, the League of Nations. The latter was founded in 1919 after the catastrophic events of the First World War and was based in Geneva. Its main objective was to promote peace and international cooperation in the wake of the earlier devastation. It was through the League of Nations that Britain had acquired the mandate over Palestine in 1922; it was this mandate, after all, that paved the way for the ultimate establishment of a homeland for the Jews, in fulfilment of some of the promises of the 1917 Balfour Declaration.

The UN was not only a useful forum in which to discuss the problems in Palestine; it was also the 'ultimate' international body whose many agencies carry international legitimacy and where nation-states put forward their national views to secure international approval for their policies and actions—political, economic, environmental, scientific, medical, financial and many others.

The problems associated with the crisis in Palestine found a niche in the international forum of the UN. The Arab and Muslim world relied on it to obtain political gain for the Palestinians. It was the one place where they could interact on a quasi-informal basis with representatives of other countries and lobby for Arab rights.

This chapter illustrates the changes that took place in the UN after the 1973 Arab–Israeli war. It demonstrates the impact of linkage strategy on international affairs, and points out the differences in the international arena of the Palestinian case in a before-and-after manner: before the war, the problem was restricted to one of refugees; after the war, it became one of self-determination, human rights and sovereignty.

In a measure of the extent of linkage through the UN, Saudi Arabia was one of the fifty-one original signatories to the UN charter in October 1945. This network of links through the UN also took on a personal form: Ahmad Shukairy, a Palestinian official later to become the first leader of the PLO, was the Saudi representative/ambassador to the UN from 1957 to 1962.

THE QUESTION OF PALESTINE

The UN has been a useful barometer of the tri-polar relationship between the Gulf, the Palestine problem and the USA. It provided a space where the three interacted, and is a convenient domain within which to view the interaction. Its activities provide a consensus on the nature of the Palestine problem.

The starting point should be the General Assembly, which meets annually and has an almost universal membership. It is a place where countries are obliged, often annually, to take a public position on major issues by voting or abstaining. Naturally, countries that are the least concerned with specific issues are the most likely to be swayed for or against them, depending on political or economic circumstances.[3] This does not however mean that they are obligated to act on the issue at hand.

Because of the international status and regular meetings of the General Assembly, it has been there where so many resolutions on Palestine have been made. The earliest Gulf–Palestine linkage at the UN probably occurred in 1945 when Prince Faisal ibn Abdel Aziz attended the San Francisco meetings to set up the UN. He was also one of the first signatories of the Declaration of Human Rights.

The UN legitimised the state of Israel. In 1947, General Assembly Resolution 181 agreed on the partition of Palestine and in 1949, the General Assembly voted to accept Israel as a member state of the UN. Throughout the intervening years, despite attempts by different Arab states to change the perception of Palestine from a refugee problem to one of rights, little headway was made.

In 1947, the UK representative at the UN had asked the organisation to place the 'Question of Palestine' on the agenda of the General Assembly: this title included such as items as termination of the mandate, assistance to refugees, status of Jerusalem, repatriation or resettlement of refugees and others, and continued to be discussed as such in the General Assembly until 1951 when it was dropped from the agenda by Secretary-General Trygve Lie.

A glance at the names of the resolutions of the General Assembly (listed in a note at the end of this chapter) during the years following 1949 reveals the nature of the discussions. Assistance to Palestinian refugees dominated the resolutions.[4]

Until the introduction of linkage strategy, therefore, the question of Palestine as viewed and debated by the international community was primarily one of refugees. There was a cursory interest in the issue of human rights: Resolution 2546 on human rights, moreover, was only introduced after the invasion and occupation of the West Bank and Gaza during the 1967 war and was applicable to all peoples under occupation. The same can be said of Resolution 2649, which asserted the rights of people to self-determination. The annual resolutions that debated on Israeli practices were also in response to the military occupation.

The many resolutions on the UN Relief and Works Agency for Palestine Refugees in the Near East (UNRWA) were in stark contrast to other, concurrent workings of the General Assembly. In 1960, for example, different resolutions were passed admitting the Togolese Republic to membership of the UN, the same year that membership was voted for the Malagasy Republic, Somalia, Congo (Léopoldville), Congo (Brazzaville), Dahomey, the Niger, Upper Volta, the Ivory Coast, the Central African Republic, Mali and Nigeria. The next year, Sierra Leone, the Mongolian People's Republic and Mauritania were admitted as members. In 1962, new members admitted by General Assembly resolutions included Burundi, Rwanda, Jamaica and Trinidad and Tobago.

There were no moves whatsoever to grant the Palestinians membership at this time. Their persistent position as refugees, reflected in the annual report of the director of UNRWA, was reinforced by the annual extension of UNRWA's mandate. After the 1967 war, another status was added in parallel with that of refugees: the Palestinians were regarded as people living in occupied territories.

A major change was immediately apparent after 1973. The European Community recognised the fact that an Arab–Israeli peace agreement should take account of the legitimate rights of the Palestinians, and the US government recognised that a settlement should include consideration of the legitimate interests of the Palestinians and had made its view known that a peace agreement must recognise that Jerusalem contained two places considered holy by the three monotheistic religions.[5]

Resolution 3175, adopted on 17 December 1973, affirmed the right of the Arab people to permanent sovereignty over their national resources in the occupied Arab territories; and for the first time since 1952, the question of Palestine was returned to its former place on the agenda of the General Assembly.

Another major departure was the international recognition of the PLO as the sole representatives of the Palestinians. This was formalised in Resolution 3210 (October 1974), which considered the Palestinians to be the principal party to the question of Palestine. It invited the PLO, as the representative of the Palestinian people, to participate in the deliberations of the General Assembly in plenary meetings on the question of Palestine. The PLO, which had been an international outcast, was now recognised as a legitimate organisation. On 13 November 1974, Yasser Arafat addressed the UN in a plenary session, the first representative of a liberation movement, rather than a member state, to do so.

Resolution 3376 (1975) established a Committee on the Exercise of the Inalienable Rights of the Palestinian People. This took place on 10 December 1975, and consisted of twenty member states. Its functions were to recommend a programme for the implementation of the rights of the Palestinian people. Every year, a similar resolution is adopted under the agenda item 'The Question of Palestine'. Resolution 3379 (1975) on the elimination of all forms of racial discrimination determined that Zionism is a form of racism. This resolution remained in force until it was revoked in 1991, when the international political standing of the PLO had reached its lowest ebb as a result of its stand during and after the 1990 Iraqi invasion of Kuwait. The resulting loss of support for the Palestinians by the Gulf states strained their relationship.

Palestine was no longer confined to being a refugee problem. Its people were recognised by the UN and other international organisations as having legitimate political rights. Their self-determination and inalienable rights became accepted principals in the international arena.[6] It was grudgingly accepted almost worldwide that no peace settlement could take place without Palestinian participation and an acceptance of their legitimate rights.

Accordingly, the PLO was invited to participate in efforts for peace in the Middle East (Resolution 3375, 1975). It also participated in official meetings of the Security Council on 5 December 1975 when it was granted the same rights as other participants of the Council.

THE SECURITY COUNCIL

The question of Palestine had been an item for discussion in the Security Council from 1947 to 1967: the topics discussed were Israeli violations of the Armistice Agreement, complaints by Egypt, Syria and Jordan of attacks on their borders, etc. After the 1967 war, 'The Question of Palestine' was removed and replaced by 'The Middle East Situation'.[7]

Security Council resolutions are more binding than those of the General Assembly. They therefore carry greater weight. The USA has vetoed resolutions deploring and condemning Israeli practices with noteworthy frequency. It has already been mentioned that King Faisal felt personally thwarted by the US veto of the July 1973 resolution (S/10974) deploring Israel's continuing occupation of territories. The prominent use of the US veto continued unabated despite the 1973 war. The draft resolution had been submitted by Guinea, India, Indonesia, Kenya, Panama, Peru, Sudan and Yugoslavia. It had reaffirmed S/242, adding that a just and peaceful solution could only be achieved through respect for the national sovereignty, territorial integrity and rights of all states in the region, as well as the rights and legitimate aspirations of the Palestinians. Although Britain and France voted for it, the USA refused to do so, the only country that voted against it.[8]

Initially, the USA had not vetoed Security Council resolution 338 (October 1973) which called on all parties to implement the provisions of S/242, and which also called for urgent negotiations to establish a just and durable peace. At this point, during and immediately after the war, it was unhesitating in its statements about Palestinian rights. In his opening remarks during the Geneva peace talks in December 1973, Kissinger as US secretary of state stated that a peace agreement must include 'a settlement of the legitimate interests of the Palestinians, and a recognition that Jerusalem contains places considered holy by three great religions'.[9]

This was echoed by the EC, whose joint statement in November 1973 recognised that the legitimate rights of the Palestinians had to be taken into account if a peace agreement was to be durable.

But once the urgency of the war and the oil boycott had passed, the US government once again adopted a strong anti-Palestinian stand. It vetoed

- resolution S/11898 (1975) condemning Israeli air raids on Lebanon and Palestinian refugee camps;
- resolution S/11940 (1976) affirming the inalienable rights of the Palestinians to self-determination, national independence and return to their homes;
- resolution S/12022 (1976) deploring Israel's failure to stop actions changing the status of Jerusalem and calling on it to desist from land expropriations and settlements;
- resolution S/13911 (1980) affirming the inalienable rights of the Palestinians to self-determination, national independence and return to their homes;
- resolution S/14943 (1982) denouncing Israel's dismissal of Palestinian elected officials and other human rights violations;
- resolution S/15895 (1983) calling Israeli settlements in the West Bank illegal and deploring settlement building;
- resolution S/17459 (1985) deploring Israeli repressive practices against civilian populations;
- resolution S/17769 (1986) deploring provocative acts by the Israelis which violate the sanctity of the Haram al-Sharif in Jerusalem;
- resolution S/20463 (1989) deploring Israeli policies towards Palestinians in the Occupied Territories; and others.[10]

It is obvious that the post-1973 linkage strategy had a marked impact on the General Assembly, but only a limited effect on the Security Council because of US government vetoes which prevented the international organisation from altering the status quo regarding Israel.

The USA did make some concessions regarding Palestinian rights and interests as a result of the oil embargo. Security Council resolution 338 (October 1973), which passed by unanimous vote,[11] called on all the parties concerned to implement S/242 and for urgent negotiations to establish a just and durable peace. There were other US concessions. The presence of the PLO in UN meetings was, for example, grudgingly accepted. For the first time, the deliberations on the question of Palestine included recognised Palestinian participation. The PLO remained an outlawed organisation as far as the USA was concerned, but its participation in the General Assembly, the Security Council and other UN bodies such as UNESCO, UNICEF etc. was tolerated.

When Yasser Arafat addressed the General Assembly in New York in 1974, the USA granted him and his entourage entry visas. They were confined to a few miles around New York City, but they were allowed in all the same. In 1988, when the political situation had altered dramatically and the PLO was living ignominiously in exile in Tunisia, Arafat was categorically refused a US visa to address the UN. As a result, he was obliged to go to Geneva to address a specially convened UN meeting. The triangular relationship had altered in shape and structure; this was clearly reflected in official US attitude to the PLO.

The General Assembly has had twenty-eight 'special sessions' during its lifetime. The first two were concerned with Palestine. The first, in 1947, was convened by Britain. The second, in 1948, was convened by the Security Council. The twenty-eighth, convened on 24 January 2005, was a commemoration of the sixtieth anniversary of the liberation of the Nazi concentration camps. Others included the Earth Summit (1997), Women 2000 (2000) and AIDS (2001). Palestine was never brought up again.

The General Assembly also has emergency sessions. Such sessions are held when 'new conditions are being created on the ground'. For example, the tenth emergency session was held on 5 February 1999 to consider 'Illegal Israeli Actions in Occupied East Jerusalem and the rest of the Occupied Palestinian Territory'. In December 2003 an emergency session on Palestine was called for to adopt a General Assembly resolution to ask the International Court of Justice to render an opinion on the 'legal consequences arising from the construction of the wall being built by Israel, the occupying Power, in the Occupied Palestinian Territory, including in and around East Jerusalem'.

UN RESOLUTIONS CONCERNING PALESTINE: 1949–1973

Resolution 302: Assistance to Palestine Refugees (1949);
Resolution 393: Assistance to Palestine Refugees (1950);
Resolution 394: Palestine: Progress Report of United Nations Conciliation for Palestine Refugees and Payment of Compensation Due to Them (1950);
Resolution 513: Assistance to Palestine Refugees (1952);
Resolution 614: Report of Director of United Nations Relief and Works Agency for Palestine Refugees in the Near East (1952);
Resolution 720: Report of Director of United Nations Relief and Works Agency for Palestine Refugees in the Near East (1953);
Resolution 818: Report of Director of United Nations Relief and Works Agency for Palestine Refugees in the Near East (1954);
Resolution 916: Report of Director of United Nations Relief and Works Agency for Palestine Refugees in the Near East (1955);
Resolution 1018: Report of Director of United Nations Relief and Works Agency for Palestine Refugees in the Near East (1957);
Resolution 1191: Report of Director of United Nations Relief and Works Agency for Palestine Refugees in the Near East (1957);
Resolution 1315: Report of Director of United Nations Relief and Works Agency for Palestine Refugees in the Near East (1958);
Resolution 1456: Report of Director of United Nations Relief and Works Agency for Palestine Refugees in the Near East (1959);

Resolution 1725: Report of Director of United Nations Relief and Works Agency for Palestine Refugees in the Near East (1961);
Resolution 1856: Report of Director of United Nations Relief and Works Agency for Palestine Refugees in the Near East (1962);
Resolution 1912: Report of Director of United Nations Relief and Works Agency for Palestine Refugees in the Near East (1963);
Resolution 2002: Extension of the Mandate of the United Nations Relief and Works Agency for Palestine Refugees in the Near East (1965);
Resolution 2052: Report of Director of United Nations Relief and Works Agency for Palestine Refugees in the Near East (1965);
Resolution 2154: Report of Director of United Nations Relief and Works Agency for Palestine Refugees in the Near East (1966);
Resolution 2341: Report of Director of United Nations Relief and Works Agency for Palestine Refugees in the Near East (1967);
Resolution 2443: Respect for and Implementation of Human Rights in Occupied Territories (1968);
Resolution 2452: Report of Director of United Nations Relief and Works Agency for Palestine Refugees in the Near East (1968);
Resolution 2535: United Nations Relief and Works Agency for Palestine Refugees in the Near East (1969);
Resolution 2546: Respect for and Implementation of Human Rights in Occupied Territories (1969);
Resolution 2628: The Situation in the Middle East (1970);
Resolution 2649: The Importance of the Universal Realisation of the Rights of People to Self-Determination and of the Speedy Granting of Independence to Colonial Countries and Peoples for the Effective Guarantee and Observance of Human Rights (1970);
Resolution 2656: Establishment of Working Group on the Financing of United Nations Relief and Works Agency for Palestine Refugees in the Near East (1970);
Resolution 2727: Report of the Special Committee to Investigate Israeli Practices Affecting the Human Rights of the Population of the Occupied Territories (1970);
Resolution 2728: Report of Working Group on the Financing of United Nations Relief and Works Agency for Palestine Refugees in the Near East (1970);
Resolution 2791: Working Group on the Financing of United Nations Relief and Works Agency for Palestine Refugees in the Near East (1971);
Resolution 2792: United Nations Relief and Works Agency for Palestine Refugees in the Near East (1971);
Resolution 2851: Report of the Special Committee to Investigate Israeli Practices Affecting the Human Rights of the Population of the Occupied Territories (1971);
Resolution 2963: United Nations Relief and Works Agency for Palestine Refugees in the Near East (1972);

90 Palestine and the Gulf States

Resolution 2964: Working Group on the Financing of United Nations Relief and Works Agency for Palestine Refugees in the Near East (1972);

Resolution 3089: United Nations Relief and Works Agency for Palestine Refugees in the Near East (1973);

Resolution 3090: Working Group on the Financing of United Nations Relief and Works Agency for Palestine Refugees in the Near East (1973);

Resolution 3092: Report of the Special Committee to Investigate Israeli Practices Affecting the Human Rights of the Population of the Occupied Territories (1973).

8 The 1990s

The Iraqi invasion of Kuwait on 2 August 1990 was a defining moment in the modern history of the Gulf. It marked the end of one era and the beginning of another concerning the linkages and relationships between Palestine and the Gulf. The occupation of one Arab country by another unleashed some dormant forces and gave rise to totally new ones. The result was the polarisation of the entire Arab world.

The invasion underlined the strong connection between Palestine and the Gulf, perhaps for the first time in the public arena. Ultimately, however, it also led to a serious rupture in the relationship. New forces were unleashed throughout the Arab world which could not be contained.

Iraq had overlooked one fact in the heat and rush of the invasion: Kuwaiti sovereignty had been underlined, accepted and guaranteed by the member states of international and regional institutions, such as the United Nations and the Arab League. These two bodies and all their attendant organisations had accepted Kuwait as a fully independent, sovereign state when it achieved its independence from Britain in 1961. As a member of both bodies, Iraq had also formally acknowledged this.

For the first time since the early nineteenth century a serious attempt was made to dismantle the state system that Britain had established and maintained so assiduously over the long years. The Iran–Iraq war, which had engaged the two military giants of the region in mortal combat, had left the Gulf states largely unscathed. This attested to the strength and durability of Britain's legacy, which endured well after its withdrawal. The invasion of Kuwait was the first major challenge to this system, and its gravity was reflected in the international response, led by Britain and the USA, which was swift and uncompromising.

In the Arab world, the response was mixed. Egypt and Syria rallied to the side of Kuwait from the earliest days of the crisis, and later sent forces to join the international military force in expelling Iraq from Kuwait. Together with the six GCC countries, they constituted what became known as the Damascus Declaration, originally intended to become a new and independent multilateral defence alliance. It called for closer cooperation between the GCC states, which would be bolstered by Syrian and Egyptian military power. Nothing came of this, although it did contribute to increasing polarisation within the Arab world.

Other Arab countries were strongly opposed to the use of Western soldiers to eject Iraq from Kuwait, but were unable to provide a viable alternative. Popular feelings ran high throughout the Arab world, particularly when contrasts were drawn between US acquiescence of the continuing Israeli occupation of Palestinian territory and its decisive response to the Iraqi occupation of Kuwait in January 1991.

No Arab leader was strong enough to prevent the divisions that spread across the region. Many Arabs were struck by what they regarded as the double standards that allowed the West to turn a blind eye to Israeli occupation while being prepared to go to war because of Iraqi occupation. Many others condemned the occupation of Kuwait in a two-wrongs-don't-make-a-right response.

The PLO was unaware of the dangers of the course it was about to follow. It was swept along by the strong emotions provoked in many Arab capitals by the double standards that led to the international reaction to the occupation of Kuwait, while its own territory was occupied with impunity. The organisation reacted with an anger born of frustration at the ongoing situation of its people.

It first registered this anger in a meeting of Arab League foreign ministers hurriedly called for 3 August. The meeting condemned Iraqi aggression and called for immediate and unconditional withdrawal; it also rejected foreign intervention and called for an Arab summit to facilitate a negotiated settlement. The PLO unwisely abstained from this resolution, which was passed by fourteen of the twenty-one representatives there. The next day, at a meeting of the Organisation of the Islamic Conference (OIC), a vote was taken to condemn the Iraqi action; again, the PLO refrained.

The Arab summit took place on 10 August. It rejected the Iraqi annexation of Kuwait, and called for the immediate restoration of the Kuwaiti government. It also supported the right of the Gulf states to self-defence, a clear mark of approval for the growing international movement regarding the use of force to restore Kuwaiti sovereignty. The PLO this time voted against the resolution. The Kuwaiti government, together with those of other Gulf states, regarded this as betrayal; the hurt was compounded by the many years of Gulf support for the Palestinian cause and, more recently, for the PLO.

These three meetings sealed the fate of the Palestinians for many years to come. The PLO made several attempts during the coming weeks to improve its standing vis-à-vis the Gulf states. Abu Iyyad, the organisation's second-in-command, stated that it was unacceptable to seize territory by force. Other PLO officials made similar statements to soften the impression it had made during those three early meetings, but the feeling throughout the world, supported by its continuing failure to condemn the invasion, was that the PLO was somehow supporting the occupation of Kuwait.

The PLO position was further compromised when, on 12 August, Saddam Hussein made a new and desperate attempt to extricate his country from the impasse he had created for it: he linked Iraqi withdrawal from Kuwait to Israeli withdrawal from the West Bank and Gaza, from the Golan and from southern Lebanon. He offered to withdraw his army from Kuwait if Israel would withdraw from Arab land. This Iraqi 'initiative' was totally disregarded internationally, and had little impact on Iraq's political position. The PLO, in the mean time, continued to weaken as the US-led multinational forces prepared for military action.

The PLO's iconic moment was a photograph of Arafat embracing and kissing Saddam; this image was beamed to TV stations the world over, and led to further isolation. In reality, Arafat did attempt to pursue a neutral path after the initial Arab League meetings. He tried to contain the problem within the Arab world, and attempted the narrow course of seeking to neutralise and defuse the conflict. He obviously had little concept of the international significance of the situation and, like Saddam Hussein, was hampered by his narrow perspective.

The PLO lacked the institutional depth to gauge the long-term results of its actions. It also lacked the tools to assess the sixty years of unbroken links between Palestine and the Gulf; this would have alerted it to the disastrous consequences of its policy.

One of the most obvious and immediate of these was the wave of anger that swept the Gulf states. They felt betrayed by the PLO's failure to fully support them in their moment of crisis. Arafat himself became a very unpopular figure throughout the region. In the mean time, as the USA was gathering a large multinational force to evict Iraq from Kuwait, the PLO became increasingly ostracised, and viewed as an ally of the invading country.

Another serious consequence for the Palestinians was the mass exodus of refugees from the Gulf states, which affected the Palestinians working and living in the region—along with millions of other expatriates, who were forced to leave as a result of the conflict. In Kuwait alone, there were at least 400,000 Palestinians who had formed a thriving community. The PLO policies impacted dramatically on their situation. Regarded by the Kuwaitis as traitors because of the misguided attitude of their leaders, they inevitably became scapegoats.

Aware that they would be held responsible for the actions of the PLO, they fled the country. They went overland, since there were no other means of transport out of Kuwait. It was high summer in the Gulf, and they travelled across the scorching desert with all their possessions cramped into different-sized vehicles. Their destination was Jordan, where many had relatives and friends and where there was a large Palestinian population; Jordan was also the transit point for Gaza and the West Bank. On reaching the border, they were stopped by the Jordanian authorities for processing. This lasted many months: in a depressingly familiar scene, they were packed into tents, which were hurriedly put up and had only minimal standards of health and sanitation.

The whole episode was devastating for the Palestinians. Their communities in Kuwait and the other Gulf states were decimated. Their economic situation was also disastrous. They had fled with little money, and had few prospects for employment elsewhere, either in Jordan or the West Bank.

The Palestinians of the West Bank and Gaza were of course in a much worse situation. The intifada had radically cut per capita income, and remittances from the Gulf had become increasingly vital to economic survival. The Iraqi invasion brought an abrupt end to this source of income, adding to the general level of destitution. Most other sources of income from the Gulf also ceased. In Kuwait, for example, the government had authorised the PLO to collect a 5 per cent tax from Palestinians working there, estimated at $50 million per annum. This was discontinued as a result of the mass exodus of expatriate Palestinians. Yet another large and devastating consequence impacted on the large sums of money regularly donated from Gulf governments, institutions and individuals to Palestine.

The accumulation of these catastrophic events led to the marginalisation of the PLO in Arab and international affairs. It lost its basic financial support of $72 million per annum from Saudi Arabia and $48 million from Kuwait. It is known that the PLO lost at least 80 per cent of its funding as a result of the Gulf war. It had to implement stringent financial measures to survive; this included a reduction in the number of its offices abroad, and the laying off of some of its employees. In March 1993, it was forced to close three of its own departments: Culture, Information and Social Affairs.

After the defeat of Saddam Hussein's forces and the restoration of the Kuwaiti state as a result of the battles of Desert Storm, the rupture of the Palestinians' relationship with the Gulf was almost complete. This was emphasised by the murder of Abu Iyyad on 15 January 1991. He had been openly opposed to linking the Iraqi invasion to the problem of Palestine, and could well have salvaged the organisation politically had he lived. Saddam Hussein was known to have been furious with his stance against the invasion, and is said to have thrown the Palestinian official out of his office when he visited him in an effort to delink with Iraq.[1]

The Palestine question lost its international focus as a result of the PLO's attitude throughout the crisis. There were some moves to keep the issue alive, but these were neither initiated nor introduced by the PLO itself. In July 1991, for example, King Fahd endorsed President Mubarak's call for an end to the boycott of Israel by the Arab League in exchange for an end to the building of Jewish settlements in the West Bank. But such moves were minor, and did not in any way alleviate the increasingly acute plight of the Palestinians. The US Department of State reported in March 1991 that Soviet Jews were settling in the West Bank and Gaza at a higher rate than reported by the Israeli government, and that the Jewish population there was growing at 10 per cent annually.

Arafat was intensely aware of US policy and how it was undermining the possibility of a future Palestinian state. Talk of an international conference began to circulate in the chanceries of the world in direct response to official Arab calls for an equitable solution to the Palestine problem after the reversal of the Iraqi invasion of Kuwait. These calls reflected the many popular demonstrations that had taken place in Arab countries condemning the hypocrisy of their governments in the immediate aftermath of the Iraqi invasion.

The PLO endorsed the holding of an international conference on Palestine which would include it as a participant. Yitzhak Shamir, the Israeli prime minister, vowed that his country would never take part in an international conference. As the issue became more hotly contested in the media, Arab governments were finding it difficult to contain the murmurings of their people about double standards.

In the meantime, President Bush presented his goals for US policy in the Middle East to a joint session of Congress in early March 1991. Two of the four objectives were closely linked: Gulf security and an Arab–Israeli peace. Bush was under pressure to deliver some sort of solution after the violence of Desert Storm had ended in an unparalleled US victory. He quietly urged the Israelis to desist from building settlements in the Occupied Territories, and to accept the growing concept of an end to the boycott in exchange.

In a bid to contain the expanding rate of Jewish settlements in the West Bank, which were fast becoming a fait accompli and which preempted negotiations, Bush asked Congress to delay considering $10 billion loan guarantees to Israel for three months. This was accepted, and in early October, the US Senate formally agreed to his request. Despite this move, Israel obtained a great advantage at almost the same time: the restoration of diplomatic ties with the USSR, which had ruptured after the June 1967 war.

On 30 October 1991, the Madrid Peace Conference took place under the joint auspices of the USA and the USSR. Although the latter was officially a convener of the conference, it was then in free fall and about to disintegrate. There can be no doubt whatsoever that the conference was a US event, a fact that prompted the Popular Front for the Liberation of Palestine (PFLP) faction, led by George Habash, to suspend its membership of the PLO executive committee. Its reasoning was that Israel had always wanted the USA to be the sole arbiter of the problem, and that in accepting the conference, the PLO was thereby promoting a long-term Israeli strategic objective. Israel refused to negotiate directly with the PLO: the Palestinians acquiesced, and attended as part of a joint Jordanian delegation. The other delegations were those of Egypt, Syria, Lebanon and Israel.

The PLO had suffered so many blows as a result of its political stance following the Iraqi invasion that it had little to fall back on. There would be no independent Palestinian delegation; and the PLO would not be officially represented despite its 1988 recognition of Israel and renunciation of terrorism. The long years of attempting to obtain official recognition had come to nothing in the face of the new world order that the USA had created. USSR involvement was little more than a façade.

The conference was to establish a new framework for the question of Palestine. The Palestinian delegation agreed *ipso facto* to opt out of the UN system and to acquire a different benchmark for future negotiations. The UN-based principles of land for peace were no longer the points of reference. This was underlined by the fact that the UN secretary-general's representative to the conference was a mere observer, and not a participant. The PLO lost the backing of the international organisation whose legality was universally acknowledged and whose various bodies had consistently upheld the rights of the Palestinians. The hard work invested in the UN system was thereby relinquished. The PLO was now in the precarious position of being under US tutelage. In the coming years, its stance was to lead to the legitimisation of the Israeli occupation.

Another long-term Israeli objective had been direct bilateral negotiations with the different Arab countries. This was also achieved at the Madrid conference with the establishment of national negotiating teams empowered and authorised to communicate and engage in dialogue with Israel.

The GCC was invited to send a representative as an observer, and to participate in organising negotiations on multilateral issues. The Saudi ambassador to the USA, Prince Bandar bin Sultan, who had been directly involved in the run-up to the conference, made a surprise appearance at the conference, which he was officially attending as a member of the GCC delegation.

Palestinian and Israeli delegates began meetings under US auspices. Although the PLO was not officially a part of the Palestinian delegation, it was clearly directing the talks behind the scenes. An Israeli objection regarding procedural matters was removed at this time: the inclusion of Diaspora Palestinians as members of negotiating teams to discuss economic development and refugee issues.

Israel soon began to reap the benefits of the new framework. In October 1992, Congress approved a foreign aid package for Israel, including the $10 billion guarantee that had earlier been withheld. France pledged $500 million in loan guarantees to build housing for immigrants. There were also diplomatic and political gains: besides having restored diplomatic relations with the USSR, Israel now began a new form of relationship with China whereby the deputy foreign minister made his first trip to Israel—the most senior member of the government ever to go there. Also, Zambia renewed its diplomatic ties, the European Community provided Israel with a $200 million subsidy, and India announced the establishment of diplomatic relations.

THE 1993 OSLO AGREEMENTS

The situation in the West Bank and Gaza had been dire since the intifada began in 1987. It worsened after the occupation of Kuwait, as seen above. The financial and diplomatic losses of the PLO were compounded by the increasingly fraught conditions of day-to-day life. In March 1991, for example, the Israeli government imposed a new set of restrictions on the Palestinians: workers were forbidden to drive their own vehicles into Israel. House demolitions continued, together with deportations and assassinations. In July 1991, the thousandth Palestinian was killed since the beginning of the intifada, and in September, the Israeli army arrested 463 people accused of being PFLP activists. In 1991 alone, there was a 62 per cent increase in killings of Palestinians by the Israeli army. Later that year, Israeli settlers invaded Silwan outside Jerusalem, occupying Arab homes. In March 1992, the Israeli government imposed a military closure on the West Bank with checkpoints: Palestinians were denied entry to Israel and access to Jerusalem, thus depriving thousands of workers of their livelihoods. And at the end of 1992, Israel expelled 415 Palestinians from Gaza and the West Bank to Lebanon, where they were to languish in shocking conditions for many months.

Within the context of these events, and its declining regional and international status, the PLO had no option but to accept the next step after the Madrid conference: the Oslo Agreements. In late August 1993, Israelis and Palestinians met in Oslo and reached a final agreement of what they named the Declaration of Principles (DOP), which was endorsed by the Fatah Central Committee in early September. Yasser Arafat then proceeded to recognise the right of Israel to exist in peace and security, and Itzhak Rabin recognised the PLO as the representative of the Palestinian people. The DOP was signed on 13 September 1993 in the White House under the auspices of President Clinton, a firm reminder of the new status of the USA as arbiter of the question of Palestine.

Once the euphoria of 'peace' was over and the dust began to settle, it became very clear that the DOP was an acknowledgement of the new weakness of the PLO and, with it, the Palestinians.

The reaction of the Gulf states is worth noting. Saudi Arabia, the dominant party, at first went along with the DOP, all the time emphasising that multilateral negotiations should be continued alongside the bilateral talks. By 1995, exasperated with Israeli intransigence, the Saudi foreign minister made a strong statement to the UN urging the two co-sponsors of the peace process to compel the Israeli government to abide by its commitments and desist from blocking the transition to the second phase of the DOP whereby their forces would be redeployed, greater power transferred to the Palestinian Authority and preparations for elections would take place.[2] Once again, he stressed that the question of Jerusalem was at the heart of the conflict. How it was handled would impact directly on the future of the peace process. He accused the Israeli authorities of continuing to take steps to change the demographic character of the city, and stressed that UN resolutions 242 and 252 (regarding Jerusalem) remained the basis of the Saudi position.

THE TRANSITION IN THE GULF

After the departure of British forces in 1971, the USA had rather timidly sought to replace them. The dual role it played throughout the Iraq–Iran war is a good example: it remained in the background, out of the limelight. It began to assert itself as a major Gulf player in 1987 when it intervened to protect Kuwaiti ships from Iranian threats. It put together a vast armada of ships from many countries (including France, Britain, Belgium, Holland, Italy and the USSR) alongside its own. The US fleet in the waters in and around the Gulf was the largest such assembly abroad since the Vietnam war: it included 30 ships—battleships, carriers, frigates, minesweepers and support vessels—and at least 30,000 men.

The 1990 events catapulted the USA to centre stage in the region. It flaunted its military might, and stormed across the Gulf in a stunning campaign, every detail of which was instantaneously beamed across the world through the newly introduced medium of satellite TV. America thereby proclaimed and confirmed its accession to hegemony of the Gulf.

In 1903, Lord Curzon (the viceroy of India) had visited the Gulf with all the pomp and ceremony of the late Victorian empire in order to confirm the supremacy of British influence there. He held Great Durbars for the different rulers. In his speech to the rulers of the then Trucial states, he proclaimed: 'We are not going to throw away this century of costly and triumphant enterprise; we shall not wipe out the most unselfish page in history. The peace of these waters must be maintained; your independence will continue to be upheld; and the influence of the British government must remain supreme.'[3]

Almost a century later, the US commander General Norman Schwarzkopf gave regular press conferences during military operations to explain the progress of the war. While these conferences were not Great Durbars, the message they conveyed echoed that of Curzon: the USA was the power that maintained the peace and guaranteed the independence and sovereignty of the Gulf states, all the while upholding its supreme influence.

As in the aftermath of the Iraq–Iran war, the basic geo-political characteristics of the region remained the same after Desert Storm. But the USA did not take long to place its imprint on the region. Two major American policies dominated the 1990s: the first was the introduction and implementation of 'dual containment' towards Iraq and Iran; the second was the introduction and implementation of a series of bilateral military and political agreements with the small Gulf states. The combination of the two inevitably impacted on linkage with Palestine.

DUAL CONTAINMENT

In 1992, Bill Clinton became president, having unexpectedly defeated George Bush in the 1991 election. Clinton was to be re-elected in 1995, thereby serving two terms and dominating the decade. His Middle East policies differed somewhat from those of his predecessor, and one of the most well known of these was what became known as the dual containment of Iran and Iraq. It was both directly and indirectly connected to policy on Palestine.

Formulated by Martin Indyk,[4] the policy sought to contain the influence of both Iran and Iraq. It differed from the policies of the 1980s, which had sought to play off one country against the other in an effort to neutralise the influence of both in the region. Dual containment focused on an enhanced containment of Iraq, manifested in sanctions and the imposition of no-fly zones, amongst others; and the active containment of Iran.

Indyk accepted that there was 'a symbiotic relationship' between a successful dual containment policy and a comprehensive Middle East peace. The rationale behind this policy was that the more successful the USA was in containing the influence of Iraq and Iran, the easier it would be to achieve a lasting Arab–Israeli peace agreement.[5] And, conversely, the more successful the USA was in achieving Arab–Israeli peace, the more isolated Iraq and Iran would be.

In the mean time, the US presence in the region began to be manifested in a new and different manner. Policies clearly demonstrated a departure from the British stricture of non-interference in internal affairs so long as its own interests were not affected. The USA did not abide by these ideas: it was to bring to the Gulf states, including Iraq, a series of objectives which were to serve as future guidelines.

A new security system was put in place to reflect US priorities. All the small states signed bilateral defence agreements with the USA which echoed the old British treaties.

Democracy was the order of the day. Elections by universal suffrage were actively encouraged. Equal rights for women were promoted. The Gulf states all had free-market economies. But their membership of the Arab League and the GCC, amongst others, caused them to adhere to principles which the USA did not entirely agree with. The best known, of course, was the adherence to the Arab boycott of Israel and Israeli goods and services.

Notes

NOTES TO CHAPTER 1

1. Mohamed Heikal, *Secret Channels: The Inside Story of Arab–Israeli Peace Negotiations*, London, 1996, pp. 8–9.
2. US Department of State, *Foreign Relations of the United States*, vol. XVIII: *Arab–Israeli Dispute, 1964–1967*. Summary, p. 5. Available at http://www.fas.org/sgp/advisory/state/frusmide.html.
3. Jacob Bercovitch and Patrick M. Regan, 'The structure of international conflict management: an analysis of the effects of intractability and mediation' *International Journal of Peace Studies* 4, 1 (January 1999).
4. Gary Sick, 'The ghost at the table', *The World Today*, February 1999.
5. The letter was dated 5 April 1945, a few days before the death of the president. It is available in Evan M. Wilson, *Decision on Palestine: How the US Came to Recognize Israel*, Stanford, 1979, Appendix K, p. 180.
6. National Archives, USA, White House Memorandum of Conversation with Crown Prince Faisal, 23 November 1957.
7. *Survival* 37, 2 (Summer 1995).
8. The most striking example of this is the HP3077, a Senate bill which attempted to control the anti-Zionist content of Middle East Studies at universities which receive federal funding.
9. Also at the White House meeting were John McCloy, who had earlier been a presidential envoy to Nasser, and Robert Anderson. For an account of this entire episode, see John D. Rockefeller, *Memoirs*, New York, 2002, pp. 272–9.
10. H. G. Balfour-Paul, The Origins of the United Arab Emirates: A Political and Social History of the Trucial States, Rosemarie Said Zahlan, London: Macmillan, 1978, *International Affairs* .55, 1 (January 1979), p.156 (emphasis mine.) It is interesting to note that H. G. Balfour-Paul went on to lecture in Gulf Studies to postgraduate students at the University of Exeter.
11. FCO/8/1387; S. Falle, British Ambassador in Kuwait, to Rt Hon. Michael Stewart, Secretary of State for Foreign and Commonwealth Affairs, 14 Jan. 1970, *Kuwait AnnualReview for 1969* (printed). I am grateful to John Peterson for pointing out this reference. Shaikh Fahd was shot dead in Kuwait by the invading Iraqi army in August 1990.
12. Available at www.welfare.org.jo.
13. Anthony H. Cordesman, *The Gulf and the Search for Strategic Stability*, Boulder, 1984, p. 269.
14. Anthony Cordesman, *The Gulf in Transition: An Introduction*. October 2000, Executive Summary, p. 56. Available online at http://www.csis.org/burke/gulf/#reports.
15. Ibid., p. 8.

NOTES TO CHAPTER 2

1. Peter Partner, *Arab Voices: The BBC Arabic Service*, London, 1988, p. 5.
2. British Library, India Office Records, L/P&S/12 (Political External Files and Collections): P.Z. 7376/36: Kuwait Intelligence Summaries, No. 13 of 1936, 1 August–30 September 1936.
3. For more details on the *majlis* movement and the 1936–9 crisis in Palestine, see Rosemarie Said Zahlan, 'The Gulf states and the Palestine problem, 1936–48', *Arab Studies Quarterly* (Winter 1981), pp. 1–21.
4. Ibid.
5. India Office, L/P&S/12/3851: P.Z. 5567/37: Political Resident to India Office, 4 August 1937.
6. FO371/21862: Minute by Rendel (in reply to Colonial Secretary's letter to the Prime Minister), 14 January 1938.
7. Trefor E. Evans (ed.), *The Killearn Diaries 1934–1946, The Diplomatic and Personal Record of Lord Killearn (Sir Miles Lampson) High Commissioner and Ambassador*, London, 1972, p. 85.
8. FO371/23269: E8086/253/25: Bullard to Foreign Office, 2 December 1939.
9. FO371/21862: Minute by Rendel (in reply to Colonial Secretary's letter to the Prime Minister), 14 January 1938.
10. FO371/21905: E738/738/25: Bullard to Foreign Office, 2 January 1938.
11. India Office, L/P&S/12: Coll. 6/67–5, Cabinet Conclusion of 22 December 1937.
12. See Rosemarie Said Zahlan, *The Origins of the United Arab Emirates*, London, 1978, p. 192. This decision was never implemented: the London conference on Palestine, the White Paper that followed and the outbreak of the Second World War all occurred in the meantime. The idea was shelved after the war, when the Buraimi dispute erupted.
13. Partner, *Arab Voices*.
14. FO371/21905: E976/661/25: Jedda Report, January 1938.
15. FO371/23269: E8086/253/25: Bullard to Foreign Office, 2 December 1939.
16. Ibid. E7409/177/25: Bullard to Foreign Office, 24 October 1939.
17. In 1938, for example, a team from the famous American *Life* magazine went to Saudi Arabia to interview the king, who had signed an oil concession with a US company. Instead of talking about the concession, Abdel Aziz spent all the time explaining his hatred of Zionism to the journalists. The article finally appeared in 1939: 'King of Arabia sells oil to US', 21 August 1939.
18. For a synopsis of these recommendations, see FO371/21908: E2338/2338/25: Annual Report for Saudi Arabia, 1937. Enclosed in Bullard to Foreign Office, 26 March 1938.
19. Ibid.
20. Ibid.
21. FO371/21862: E559/1/31: Ormsby-Gore (Colonial Secretary) to Neville Chamberlain (Prime Minister), 9 January 1938.
22. Ibid.
23. FO371/21864: Memorandum by H. L. Baggalay, Eastern Department, E6231/1/31, 12 October 1938.
24. CAB23/96: Cabinet 55 (38) Conclusion 5: Jewish Problem, 9 November 1938.
25. FO371/21883: E 6606/10/31: Lindsay, Washington DC, to Foreign Office, 3 November 1938.
26. Ibid. Foreign Office to Lindsay, Washington DC, 11 November 1938.

27. FO371/21865: E6824/1/31: Draft Conclusion of the Third Meeting of the Cabinet Committee on Palestine, 14 November 1938.
28. FO371/21869: E7678/1/31: Committee on Palestine: Draft Memorandum by Foreign Secretary, 21 December 1938.
29. FO371/39991: E6910/41/65: Minister Resident, Cairo, to Foreign Office, 1 November 1944.
30. Cmnd. 6019, 1939: White Paper on Palestine, 17 May 1939.
31. Aaron David Miller, *Search for Security: Saudi Arabian Oil and American Foreign Policy 1939–1949*, Chapel Hill, NC, 1980, p. 130.
32. Ibid.
33. US Department of State, *Foreign Relations of the United States, 1945*, vol. VIII: *The Near East and Africa*, Memorandum of conversation between the King of Saudi Arabia and President Roosevelt, February 14, 1945.
34. Wilson, *Decision on Palestine*, Appendix I, p. 178.
35. US Department of State, *Foreign Relations of the United States, 1945*, vol. VIII, Memorandum of conversation between the King of Saudi Arabia and President Roosevelt, February 14, 1945.
36. Wilson, *Decision on Palestine*, Appendix K, p. 180. The letter was dated 5 April 1945.
37. Ibid., p. 54.
38. Ibid.
39. Reported by US Consul General in Kuwait, Parker T. Hart, to the Department of State in National Archives: 886 F.2553/2–851, 8 February 1951. Hart cited ARAMCO sources for his information.
40. FO371/104411: EA 15324/8: Minute by P. Ramsbotham, 21 May 1953.
41. Ibid., EA 15324/4: Political Agent Kuwait to Foreign Office, 27 March 1953.
42. See chapter 3.

NOTES TO CHAPTER 3

1. The first example of US-instigated 'regime change' in the Arab world actually was in Syria when the CIA led a coup against Shukri al-Kuwwatli in 1949 and replaced him with Husni al-Zaim. This led to a series of coups and counter-coups which marked political life in Syria until 1970 when Hafez al-Asad came to power. For an account by one of the operatives of the 1949 coup, see Miles Copeland, *The Game of Nations*, London, 1969. For a more recent analysis of the impact of the coup in Syria, see Andrew Rathmell, *Secret War in the Middle East: The Covert Struggle for Syria, 1949–1961*, London, 1995.
2. The part of the oasis given to Abu Dhabi is known today as al-Ain (after one of the principal villages) and constitutes an important part of the UAE. It is especially significant as the oasis of which Shaikh Zayid bin Sultan, president of the UAE, was formerly the governor.
3. PRO. FO1016/522: Political Agent to Political Resident, 13 November 1956.
4. Ibid.
5. For an account of the visit, see Wilbur Crane Eveland, *Ropes of Sand: America's Failure in the Middle East*, London, 1980, pp. 209–13.
6. National Archives, Washington DC, Office of Intelligence Research, Division of Research for Near East, South Asia and Africa, 'Saudi Arabia: A Disruptive Force in Western-Arab Relations', 18 January 1956.

7. Ibid., p. 17.
8. Ibid.
9. National Archives, Department of State Central Files, 786A.OO/6–2591, 25 June 1961. Reprinted in *Foreign Relations of the US 1961 (FRUS)*, GPO, Washington DC, 1961.
10. National Archives, Memorandum of Conversation, White House, 23 September 1957, RG56, 786A.11/9–2357.
11. Fawaz A. Gerges, 'The Kennedy administration and the Egyptian–Saudi conflict in Yemen:co-opting Arab nationalism', *Middle East Journal* (Spring 1995), pp. 292–312.

NOTES TO CHAPTER 4

1. Herman Frederich Eilts, 'Arab–Israeli spillover', in J. E.Peterson (ed.), *The Politics of Middle Eastern Oil*, Washington DC, 1983, pp. 308–12.
2. Institute of Palestine Studies, *al-Watha'ik al-falestiniya al-arabiah l-am 1967* (Arab Documents on Palestine for 1967), Beirut, 1969.
3. PRO, FCO8/775: Manager, British Bank of the Middle East, Khobar branch, to Head Office, 17 June 1967. Copy enclosed in British Bank of the Middle East, London to Foreign Office, 28 June 1967.
4. FCO8/772: British Embassy, Washington DC, to Foreign Office, 24 July 1968.
5. FCO17/765. Reported by British Embassy, Jeddah, to Foreign Office, 21 November 1968.
6. See, *U.S. Official Statements: The Status of Jerusalem*, Jody Boudreault and Yasser Salaam (eds.), Institute of Palestine Studies, Washington, DC, 1992.
7. In this address Johnson emphasised five principles: mutual respect of the rights of countries to live; justice for the refugees; respect for maritime rights; the danger of the arms race; and the importance of respect for political independence and territorial integrity of all states in the region with "adequate recognition of the special interest . . . in the holy places of Jerusalem." *International Documents on Palestine, 1967*, Institute of Palestine Studies, Beirut, 1970. I am indebted to Mona Nsouli, Reference Librarian, Institute of Palestine Studies for this information.
8. For a detailed account of these events see Rosemarie Said Zahlan, 'Shades of the past: the Iraq–Kuwait dispute, 1961,' *Journal of Social Affairs* 22, 87 (2005), pp. 47–80.
9. FCO8/614: British Embassy Kuwait to Foreign Office, 10 July 1967.
10. FCO8/637: British Embassy, Kuwait, to Foreign Office, 12 November 1967.
11. FCO8/1387: Kuwait Annual Review for 1969.
12. FCO8/614: Geoffrey Arthur to Foreign Office, 1 July 1967.
13. Ibid.
14. Ibid.
15. Ibid.
16. Ibid., 13 July 1967.
17. Ibid., 20 August 1967.
18. Ibid.
19. Ibid.
20. Ibid.
21. FCO 17/773: British Embassy, Kuwait, to Foreign Office, 8 January 1969.
22. FCO8/1834: Kuwait Annual Review 1971.

23. FCO8/1299: Political Agent, Bahrain, to Political Resident, 10 December 1970.
24. FCO8/553: Foreign Office to Central British Fund for Jewish Relief and Rehabilitation, 3 November 1967.
25. FCO8/565.
26. FCO8/1012.
27. FCO8/570: Annual Report Oman 1968 with British Consul General to Political Resident, 18 July 1967.
28. FCO8/724: Political Agent, Doha, to Political Resident, 16 June 1967.
29. FCO8/843: Political Agent, Abu Dhabi, to Political Resident, 17 June 1967.
30. FCO8/44: Political Resident to Foreign Office, 23 June 1967.
31. Ibid.

NOTES TO CHAPTER 5

1. The lyrics of the song were as follows, transliterated from the Arabic: 'Kul shayy yaghni ma 'ada al-jihad, fi sabil illahi wa khidmat al-bilad. Hayyu ma'yi dunya al-kuwait. F'al yahya al-kaz wa yahya al-zayt. Sahra kuddtu ansa fiki hawa Bir Zayt. Lama ita'rrafina 'ala al-akh Muhammad al-Din sara fi biladina ra'is muhandissin. "Patrician" lakinahu amin wa 'andahu min khibrat sinin. Wa lamma shafahu Halsted sara minhu usib al-din.' Text thanks to Mona and Bahij Saba of Pittsburgh, Pennsylvania, who lived in Kuwait during those years. Kamal Nasser was murdered in Beirut in 1973 by an Israeli death squad under the leadership of Ehud Barak, a future prime minister of Israel. The song refers to Kamal Nasser's home town of Bir Zeit, and to the destructive role of General Halsted, the British-appointed controller of the Development Department whose policies were wasteful and counter productive. See Rosemarie Said Zahlan, 'Kuwaiti reconstruction revisited', *Wall Street Journal Europe*, 7 May 1991.
2. Throughout the British period, no schools, hospitals or other social services were introduced to what were then extremely poor states. The people were left to their own devices. During the 1938 reform movements in Kuwait, Bahrain and Dubai, education was an important objective, and the first three primary schools in Dubai, for example, were established by the leaders of the movement. It was not until oil revenues began to accrue during the late 1940s that the more widespread provision of education was made first in Kuwait and later in Dubai; in Bahrain, oil revenues, although very limited, were first utilised to promote schooling as early as the 1930s.
3. FCO8/1804: Annual Review of Events in Persian Gulf, 1972.
4. It is interesting to note here that many Kuwaitis at this time believed that the attack on the border police station had been encouraged by Britain in order to promote more favorable terms for oil deals from Iraq. See FCO8/1988.
5. FCO8/44: Sir Stewart Crawford, Political Resident, to Foreign Office, 23 June 1967.
6. FCO8/1734: Annual Review for Saudi Arabia 1970. It is assumed that the 'extremists' referred to here were the Palestinians who were just beginning to become mobilised after the loss of the West Bank and Gaza in 1967.
7. See, for example, Robert Baer. *Sleeping with the Devil: How Washington Sold Our Soul for Saudi Crude*. Three Rivers Press (CA), 2003.
8. *Op.cit.* [FCO8/1734]

9. FCO8/1950: Minutes of Meeting between US and British officials in Washington DC, 28 September 1973.
10. Rogers rather weakly replied that Israel had made concessions by accepting a ceasefire and indirect negotiations. See FCO8/1573: British Embassy, Jedda, to Foreign Office, 9 May 1971.
11. Ibid. Extract from Record of Talks between Parsons and Kissinger, 24–26 June 1971.
12. FCO8/1737: British Embassy, Jedda, to Foreign Office, 3 November 1971.
13. FCO8/1656: British Embassy, Kuwait, to Foreign Office, 14 July 1971.
14. FCO8/1834: Kuwait Annual Review 1971.
15. For an account of this rivalry, see Rosemarie Said Zahlan, 'Anglo-American rivalry in Bahrain, 1918–47', in Abdullah bin Khalid al-Khalifa and Michael Rice (eds.), *Bahrain through the Ages: The History*, London, 1993, pp. 567–87.
16. National Security Archive, Document 4: Department of State Memo on the Middle East, 29 June 1973. Alexander Haig, then the assistant to the president, had telephoned Theodore L. Eliot, executive secretary at the State Department, that day to tell him that President Nixon did not want Rogers to proceed with his Middle East initiative because he had had a discussion with Brezhnev the week before about the subject and was awaiting his reply.
17. Kissinger later claimed that he regretted not having supported the Rogers plan, which could have prevented the 1973 war: 'Conversation with Kissinger' (minutes of a private discussion at a brunch in the Hotel Pierre in New York on 15 June 1975 between Kissinger (secretary of state) and a group of American Jewish leaders [Philip Klutznik Group]), *Journal of Palestine Studies* 10, 3 (Spring 1981), pp. 186–95.
18. Fuad Itayim, 'Arab oil: the political dimension', *Journal of Palestine Studies* 3, 2 (Winter 1974), pp. 84–97.
19. Ibid.
20. National Security Archive, Document 10: Kissinger to White House Situation Room for delivery to President Nixon, 6 October 1973. Available at www.gwu.edu.
21. Ibid., Document 16: Memo from LSE (Lawrence S. Eagleburger) to Kissinger, 6 October 1973.
22. Described in the document as secretary of state: ibid., Document 21a.
23. Ibid., Document 21b, 9 October 1973.
24. Ibid., Document 23: Department of State, Operations Center, Middle East Task Force, Situation Report 18, 10 October 1973.
25. Described in the document as assistant to the president: ibid., Document 5, Memorandum of Conversation, 10 September 1973 and marked 'Top Secret/Sensitive. Exclusively Eyes Only'. The meeting appeared to have taken place in the White House at what Kissinger referred to in the minutes as 'this restricted channel'.
26. Ibid.
27. Ibid.
28. Ibid.
29. Ibid., Document 29a: Kissinger to Faisal (sent through the US embassy, Jiddah), 14 October 1973.
30. Ibid., Document 34b: Memorandum of Conversation, 17 October 1973.
31. 'Kissinger tape describes crises, war and stark photos of abuse', *New York Times*, 27 May 2004. This article refers to the declassification by the US National Archives on 26 May 2004 of 20,000 transcripts of telephone calls made during the Nixon administration.

32. Document 36a, Washington Special Actions Group Meeting, White House Situation Room, 17 October 1973. This is the only declassified document of the WSAG meetings available. Present at the meeting with Kissinger were representatives from the Pentagon, the State Department, the Joint Chiefs of Staff and the CIA.
33. FCO8/1970: British Embassy, Jedda, to Foreign Office, 16 October 1973 (telegram).
34. FCO8/1970: Foreign Secretary to British Embassy, Jedda, 18 October 1973 (telegram).
35. Ibid.: British Embassy, Jedda, to Foreign Office, 17 October 1973 (telegram).
36. Ibid.: British Ambassador, Abu Dhabi, to Foreign Office, 20 October 1973 (telegram).
37. Ibid.: British Ambassador, Kuwait, to Foreign Office, 17 October 1973 (telegram).
38. Ibid.: British Ambassador, Qatar, to Foreign Office, 20 October 1973 (telegram).
39. Barry Rubin, 'US policy, January–October 1973', *Journal of Palestine Studies* 3, 2 (Winter 1974), pp. 98–113.
40. Ibid.
41. National Security Archive, Document 45b: US Embassy, Jedda, to Secretary of State, 23 October 1973.
42. FCO8/1971: Haig (Jedda) to Foreign Office, 7 November 1973 (telegram).
43. National Security Archive, Document 54: Memorandum of Conversation, Herzliyya (near Tel Aviv), 22 October 1973. Present: Golda Meir, Mordechai Gazit (director of the prime minister's office), Kissinger, Peter Rodman (NSC staff).
44. Ibid.
45. In the same conversation, Golda Meir replied to this statement: 'I know what you did. Without you, I don't know where we would have been': Ibid.
46. Ibid.
47. Ibid., Document 47: General Scowcroft to Henry A. Kissinger, 23 October 1973.
48. Ibid.: Henry A. Kissinger to General Scowcroft, 23 October 1973.
49. 'US mulled seizing oil fields in '73', *Washington Post*, 1 January 2004.
50. [PRO] FCO8/1968: David Gore-Booth, Near East Department, Foreign Office, 28 August 1973.
51. FCO8/1971: Hawley (Oman) to Foreign Office (telegram), 20 November 1973.
52. Ibid.: Henderson to Foreign Office, 25 November 1973 (telegram).
53. Ibid.: Henderson to Foreign Office, 21 and 24 November 1973 (telegrams).
54. FCO8/1972: Henderson to Foreign Office, 17 December 1973 (telegram).
55. Ibrahim Sus, 'Western Europe and the October war', *Journal of Palestine Studies* 3, 2 (Winter 1974), pp. 65–83.
56. Itayim, 'Arab oil'.
57. Yusif A. Sayigh, 'Arab oil policies: self-interest versus international responsibility', *Journal of Palestine Studies* 4, 3 (Spring 1975), pp. 59–73.
58. Kissinger confirmed this in a recent TV interview, 'The House of Saud', Storyville, shown on BBC4, 30 May 2004.
59. Sayigh, 'Arab oil policies'.
60. FCO 8/2524: Annual Review of Qatar, 1974.
61. There is an interesting account of the visit to Lahore as viewed by the British government in FCO 8/2191: John Wilton (British ambassador, Kuwait) to Foreign Office, 27 February 1974.

NOTES TO CHAPTER 6

1. Rachel Bronson, 'Recall, Reagan had Riyadh to thank', *The Daily Star*, 19 June 2004.
2. Robert Scheer, 'Eyewitness: Andrew Young: lessons from a missed opportunity', *Los Angeles Times*, 12 September 1993.
3. Cordesman, *The Gulf and the Search for Strategic Stability*, p. 271.
4. Ibid., p. 256.
5. Ibid.
6. James E. Akins, 'Saudi Arabia, Soviet activities, and Gulf security', in Z. Michael Szaz (project director), *The Impact of the Iranian Events upon the Persian Gulf and United States Security*, American Foreign Policy Institute, Washington DC, 1979, pp. 89–90.
7. Josh Pollack, 'Saudi Arabia and the United States, 1931–2002', *Middle East Review of International Affairs* 16, 3 (September 2002), p. 7.
8. Ibid., p. 8.
9. Ibid., fn. 57.
10. See *The Independent*, 11 July 1987.
11. A number of documents relating to the Iran–Contra scandal have now been declassified, and can be viewed online at the Digital National Security Archive at http://nsarchive.chadwyck.com, from which much of this material has been drawn.
12. Digital National Security Archive, 'Iraqgate: Saddam Hussein, US Policy and the Prelude to the Persian Gulf War, 1980–1994', Introduction, p. 1. Available at http://nsarchive.chadwyck.com/igessayx.htm.
13. National Security Directive, ibid., July 1982.
14. Final Declaration issued by the Extraordinary Arab Summit Conference held at Amman, Hashemite Kingdom of Jordan, 17–20 Rabi I AH 1408/8–11 November 1987. A copy of the resolutions of this Summit are published in *Journal of Palestine Studies*, 17,3, pp. 176–177, (Spring, 1988).

NOTES TO CHAPTER 7

1. In 1965, for example, the British authorities in the Gulf manoeuvred the overthrow of Shaikh Saqr bin Sultan (r. 1951–65), the ruler of Sharjah, because he had refused British 'advice' to ignore an Arab League mission that had arrived in the then Trucial states. The objective of the League's mission was to offer them social and economic aid which they desperately needed. The British government was almost hysterical in its fear of the repercussions of the mission; this was related to apprehension about the possible arousal of pan-Arab sentiments in the Gulf. So when Shaikh Saqr agreed to see the visiting Arab League mission, the political agent, P. G. Balfour-Paul, arranged to have him removed from his position. Although many details of the staged coup have been removed from the files at the Public Record Office in London, enough material is available with which to understand the British role in the coup. See, for example, FO371/188523: Annual Review of the Trucial States 1965, and Balfour-Paul's statement about the arrival of the secretary-general of the Arab League, 'his pockets bulging with fictitious cheques'. He also referred to the removal of Shaikh Saqr 'by means of a family resolution and an [Royal] Air Force 'plane'. 'This was quickly followed by the return of the lost lambs [i.e. the other Trucial rulers], with the possible exception of the black sheep in Ras al Khaimah, to the fold . . . By now we were out of the tunnel and back in the sunlit, if bumpy, plains': ibid., BT1011/2.

2. Sally Morphet, 'States groups at the United Nations and growth of member states at the United Nations', in Paul Taylor and A. J. R. Groom (eds.), *The United Nations at the Millennium: The Principal Organs*, London, 2000.
3. Research Department, Foreign and Commonwealth Office, London, *United Nations: Does the Rhetoric Matter? A Case History: Palestine 1947–1983*, October 1983 (henceforth Research Department, FCO), pp. 2–3.
4. General Assembly sessions and resolutions are available at www.un.org/documents/ga.
5. Research Department, FCO, p. 29.
6. Resolution 3236 (1974) reaffirmed the inalienable rights of the Palestinians; Resolution 3237 (1974) gave observer status to the PLO to participate in the sessions and work of the General Assembly and all international conferences convened under the auspices of the General Assembly and other UN organs. Many more were to follow the next year.
7. For an illuminating article on the question of Palestine at the UN, see George J. Tomeh, 'When the UN dropped the Palestinian question', *Journal of Palestine Studies* 4, 1 (Autumn 1974), pp. 15–30.
8. China did not participate in the vote: Research Department, FCO, p. 29.
9. Ibid., p. 30.
10. Phyllis Bennis, 'Veto', *The Link* 36, 1 (January–March 2003), p. 9.
11. China did not participate: Research Department, FCO, p. 30.

NOTES TO CHAPTER 8

1. Salinger and Laurent narrate that Abu Iyyad and Arafat visited Saddam on 16 November and during this visit Abu Iyyad is said to have accused Saddam that he did not support the Palestine cause but undermines it and that his policies have destroyed the livelihood of thousands of Palestinians who live in Kuwait. It being noted that the family of Abu Iyyad was living in Kuwait at the time. Abu Iyyad is said to have also accused Saddam of supporting the renegade Abu Nidal, a sworn enemy of Fatah. Abu Iyyad was assassinated shortly thereafter by a member of Abu Nidal's organisation. This account is, apparently, only published in Arabic on the internet in chapter 10 of Pierre Salinger and Eric Laurent, *Thamarat al-Awraq: al-Mufakira al-Khafiya li Harb al-Khalij, Ru'ya Mutalia ala al-'Ad al-'Aksi lil Azma*, [The Secret Diary of the Gulf War: Knowledgeable account of the count down to the Crisis] -at http://iraq4all.dk/book/Mokfra/F-10.htm. The entire book can be read at http://vb.arabsgate.com/showthread.php?t=471979. I am indebted to Mona Nsouli and Jeanette Seraphim for this information
2. Prince Saud al-Faisal to the fiftieth Session of the General Assembly, 10 October 1995. The text of this talk is available in Anders Jerichow, *The Saudi File: People, Power, Politics*, London, 1998, pp. 267–75.
3. J. G. Lorimer, *Gazetteer of the Persian Gulf, Oman and Central Asia*, Farnborough, 1970 [Calcutta, 1915], vol. I, part 2, p. 2639.
4. A British-born, Australian-educated analyst, Indyk served as a researcher at AIPAC and then became founding director of the Washington Institute for Near East Policy. During the Clinton administration he became a senior member of the National Security Council, ambassador to Israel and a senior member of the Department of State.
5. See, for example, Martin Indyk, 'Oslo, the Middle East, and the Clinton years: successes, failures, and lessons', *Strategic Assessment* 4, 2 (August 2001).

Bibliography

Akins, James E., 'Saudi Arabia, Soviet activities, and Gulf security', in Z. Michael Szaz (project director), *The Impact of the Iranian Events upon the Persian Gulf and United States Security*, American Foreign Policy Institute, Washington DC, 1979
Balfour-Paul, H. G., '*The Origins of the United Arab Emirates: A Political and Social History of the Trucial States*, Rosemarie Said Zahlan, London: Macmillan 1978. 278 pp £10.00.' *International Affairs* 55, 1 (January 1979)
Bennis, Phyllis ,'Veto', *The Link* 36, 1 (January–March 2003)
Bercovitch, Jacob and Patrick M. Regan, 'The structure of international conflict management: an analysis of the effects of intractability and mediation', *International Journal of Peace Studies* 4, 1 (January 1999)
'Conversation with Kissinger' (minutes of a private discussion at a brunch in the Hotel Pierre in New York on 15 June 1975 between Kissinger (Secretary of State) and a group of American Jewish leaders [Philip Klutznik Group]), *Journal of Palestine Studies* 10, 3 (Spring 1981)
Copeland, Miles, *The Game of Nations*, London, 1969
Cordesman, Anthony H., *The Gulf and the Search for Strategic Stability*, Boulder, 1984
Cordesman, Anthony, *The Gulf in Transition: An Introduction*. October 2000. Available online at http://www.csis.org/burke/gulf/#reports.
Eilts, Herman Frederick, 'Arab–Israeli spillover', in J. E.Peterson (ed.), *The Politics of Middle Eastern Oil*, Washington DC, 1983, pp. 308–12
Evans, Trefor E. (ed.), *The Killearn Diaries 1934–1946, The Diplomatic and Personal Record of Lord Killearn (Sir Miles Lampson) High Commissioner and Ambassador*, London, 1972
Eveland, Wilbur Crane, *Ropes of Sand: America's Failure in the Middle East*, London, [[date missing]]
Foreign Relations of the US 1961, Washington DC, 1961
Gerges, Fawaz A., 'The Kennedy administration and the Egyptian–Saudi conflict in Yemen:co-opting Arab nationalism', *Middle East Journal* (Spring 1995)
Heikal, Mohamed, *Secret Channels: The Inside Story of Arab–Israeli Peace Negotiations*, London, 1996
Indyk, Martin, 'Oslo, the Middle East, and the Clinton years: successes, failures, and lessons', *Strategic Assessment* 4, 2 (August 2001)
Institute of Palestine Studies, *al-Watha'ik al-falestiniya al-arabiah l-am 1967* (Arab Documents on Palestine for 1967), Beirut, 1969
Itayim, Fuad, 'Arab oil: the political dimension', *Journal of Palestine Studies* 3, 2 (Winter 1974)
Jerichow, Anders, *The Saudi File: People, Power, Politics*, London, 1998

Lorimer, J. G., *Gazetteer of the Persian Gulf, Oman and Central Asia*, Farnborough, 1970 [Calcutta, 1915]

Khalilzad, Zalmay, 'The United States and the Persian Gulf: preventing regional hegemony', *Survival* 37, 2 (Summer 1995)

Miller, Aaron David, *Search for Security: Saudi Arabian Oil and American Foreign Policy 1939–1949*, Chapel Hill, NC, 1980

Morphet, Sally, 'States groups at the United Nations and growth of member states at the United Nations', in Paul Taylor and A. J. R. Groom (eds.), *The United Nations at the Millennium: The Principal Organs*, London, 2000

Partner, Peter, *Arab Voices: The BBC Arabic Service*, London, 1988

Pollack, Josh, 'Saudi Arabia and the United States, 1931–2002', *Middle East Review of International Affairs* l6, 3 (September 2002)

Rathmell, Andrew, *Secret War in the Middle East: The Covert Struggle for Syria, 1949–1961*, London, 1995

Rockefeller, John D., *Memoirs*, New York, 2002

Rubin, Barry, 'US policy, January–October 1973', *Journal of Palestine Studies* 3, 2 (Winter 1974)

Sayigh, Yusif A., 'Arab oil policies: self-interest versus international responsibility', *Journal of Palestine Studies* 4, 3 (Spring 1975)

Sick, Gary, 'The ghost at the table', *The World Today*, February 1999

Sus, Ibrahim, 'Western Europe and the October war', *Journal of Palestine Studies* 3, 2 (Winter 1974)

Tomeh, George J., 'When the UN dropped the Palestinian question', *Journal of Palestine Studies* 4, 1 (Autumn 1974)

US Department of State, *Foreign Relations of the United States, 1945*, vol. VIII: *The Near East and Africa*

US Department of State, *Foreign Relations of the United States*, vol. XVIII: *Arab–Israeli Dispute, 1964–1967*. Available at http://www.fas.org/sgp/advisory/state/frusmide.html.

Wilson, Evan M., *Decision on Palestine: How the US Came to Recognize Israel*, Stanford, 1979

Zahlan, Rosemarie Said, 'Anglo-American rivalry in Bahrain, 1918–47', in Abdullah bin Khalid al-Khlaifa and Michael Rice (eds.), *Bahrain through the Ages: The History*, London, 1993

Zahlan, Rosemarie Said, 'The Gulf states and the Palestine problem, 1936–48', *Arab Studies Quarterly* (Winter 1981)

Zahlan, Rosemarie Said, 'Kuwaiti reconstruction revisited', *Wall Street Journal Europe*, 7 May 1991

Zahlan, Rosemarie Said, *The Origins of the United Arab Emirates*, London, 1978

Zahlan, Rosemarie Said, 'Shades of the past: the Iraq–Kuwait dispute, 1961,' *Journal of Social Affairs* 22, 87 (2005)

Index

A
Abdel, Aziz, King of Saudi Arabia 3–4, 8, 18–25, 25, 27, 28–9, 34, 68, 102
Abu Dhabi 48
Abu Iyyad 92, 94, 109
Abu Musa 48
Abu Nidal 109
Afghanistan 68–9, 73
Agnew, Spiro 51–2, 55, 57
air traffic 5, 6; Britain's information links with Bahrain 43
airlift to Israel 53–4, 55
Akins, James 73
Albright, Madeleine 7, 27
Algiers agreement 49
American Israel Public Affairs Committee (AIPAC) 74
Anderson, Robert 32
anti-war demonstrations 6–7
Arab Bank 63
Arab Boycott Office 43
Arab Higher Committee 16, 19
Arab–Israeli Wars 2, 25–6; 1967 36–46; 1973 47–64
Arab League 49, 66, 72, 79, 91, 92, 99, 108
Arab linkage strategy 81–2
Arab militarisation 1–2
Arab Summmit of 1991 92
Arafat, Yasser 12, 50, 63, 64, 85, 87–8, 93, 95, 97, 109
ARAMCO 25, 29, 37, 60
arms sales 72–5
Arthur, Geoffrey 41–2
al-Asad, Hafez 78, 80, 103
Ashura riots 67
Aswan Dam 30
al-Atiyah, Khalifah 31

AWACS 74

B
al-Badr, Muhammad 35
Baghdad Pact 30
Bahrain 18, 48, 57, 64; reactions to 1967 war 42–3
Bakr, Ahmad Hasan 66
Balfour Declaration (1917) 5, 12, 19, 83
Balfour-Paul, H.G. 10, 101, 108
Ball, George 37–8
Ballata refugee camp 79
Banca Nazionale del Lavoro 77
Bandar bin Sultan 75, 96
Bandung Conference (1955) 30
banks, run on 41
Barak, Ehud 105
Bari radio station 16
Baroody, Jamil 51
Benhima, Ahmad Tibi 55
Bercovitch, J. 2
Berger, Sandy 7
bilateral agreements 98–9
bin Abdallah, Ali 31
bin Ghubash, Sayf 69
bin Sultan, Shaikh Zayid 44–5, 48, 56–7, 60–1, 66, 103
Bishara, Abdullah Yacoub 40, 70
Black, Eugene 9
Bludan Conference (1937) 18, 23
Bouteflika, Abdel Aziz 55
Brezhnev, Leonid 59, 106
British Bank of the Middle East 41
Bronson, Rachel 69
Bullard, Reader 19–20, 20–1, 21–2
Buraimi dispute 28–9
Bush, George 95, 99
Bush, George W. 2, 3

C

Carter, Jimmy 68, 70, 71, 73
Carter Doctrine 71
Central Committee for the Defence of Palestine 22
Chatila camp 79
Clinton, Bill 7, 97, 99
Cohen, William 7
Cold War 47, 69
Committee on the Exercise of the Inalienable Rights of the Palestinian People 85
Contras 69, 75–6
Cordesman, Anthony 14
CSIS Gulf in Transition Project 14
Curzon, Lord 98

D

Damascus Declaration (1990) 91–2
Dayan, Moshe 70
Declaration of Principles (DOP) 97
demonstrations 6–7, 45–6, 67, 78
Desert Fox 6–7
Desert Storm 94, 95
Dhahran Air Agreement 33–4
Dinitz, Simcha 53–4
Doha police fort 44
Douglas-Home, Alec 56, 60, 62
dual containment 8, 98, 99
Dubai riots 45
Dulles, John Foster 34

E

Eban, Abba 53
Eden, Anthony 3, 7, 13, 19, 20, 31
Egypt 1, 11, 27; conflict with Saudi Arabia 33, 35; Suez War 30–3
Egyptian–Israeli peace agreement 65–6
Eilts, Herman 38
Eisenhower, Dwight D. 4, 32, 33, 34
Eisenhower Doctrine 33
Eliot, Theodore L. 106
Europe 61–4, 82–3
European Community (EC) 55–6, 61, 62, 85, 86; Venice Declaration 2, 15, 70–1
Eveland, Wilbur 32
Evil Empire concept 69
Extraordinary Arab Summit, Amman 78–9

F

Fahd bin Ahmad, Shaikh 12, 40–1, 101
Fahd, King of Saudi Arabia 56, 66, 72, 94
Fahd Plan 2, 72
Faisal ibn Abdel Aziz, King of Saudi Arabia 4, 9, 32, 34–5, 36–7, 38–9, 49, 50–1, 52–3, 55, 58, 60, 62, 66, 73, 84, 86
Falle, Sam 42
Fatah 12, 50, 97
Fertile Crescent 11
Fez Declaration (1982) 72
financial donations 4, 12–13, 63

G

George VI, King of Britain 19, 21
Ghazi, King of Iraq 16, 18
Gore-Booth, David 60, 62
Grand Mosque (Mecca) 66–7, 78
Great Revolt (1936–9) 6, 16–17, 79
Greater Tunb 48
Gulf Cooperation Council (GCC) 7, 71–2, 96, 99

H

Habash, George 95
Haig, Alexander 106
Haikal, Hassanein 56
Hajj 78
Halsted, General 105
Hamad, Shaikh 31
Hasa 67
Hashemites 28
Heath, Edward 55
Heikal, Mohamed 1
human rights 84
Hussein, King of Jordan 50, 54
Husseini, Hajj Amin (Mufti) 16, 19, 22

I

Ibn Jiluwi 37, 67
India 15–16
Indyk, Martin 99, 109
'instant experts' 11–14
intifada 76–80
Iran: coup of 1953 27; hostage crisis 68; Islamic Revolution of 1979 27, 65; twin pillar of US policy 49
Irangate 75–6
Iraq 3, 13, 66; invasion of Kuwait 91–4
Iraq–Iran war 65, 66, 71, 75, 76–8, 91
Isa, Shaikh 43
Islamic Revolution (Iran, 1979) 27, 65
Israel 96, 97; Arab–Israeli Wars see Arab–Israeli Wars; creation of 1, 25; invasion of Lebanon 72, 79; twin pillar of US policy 8–10

J

Jabbar, Ahmad Abdul 34
al-Jabir, Shaikh Ahmad 16
Jaidah, Ali 61
Jarring, Gunnar 38
Jarring Mission 38
Jerusalem 38–9
Johnson, Lyndon B. 2, 38–9, 104
Jordan 50; refugees from the Gulf states 93–4

K

Kennedy, John F. 33–4
Khalid ibn Abdel Aziz, King of Saudi Arabia 66
Khalifah bin Hamad, Shaikh 44, 57, 60, 61, 63
Khalilzad, Zalmay 7
al-Khatib, Ahmad 39
al-Khayyal, Ambassador 34
Khomeini, Ayatollah Rouhallah 65
Khor el Odeid 20
Kissinger, Henry 9, 51, 52, 53–5, 58–9, 62, 65, 86, 106
Kuwait 12; and Great Revolt 16, 17; Iraqi invasion of 91–4; PLO 64, 94; reactions to 1967 war 39–42; reactions to Suez War 31
Kuwait State Office 45
al-Kuwwatli, Shukri 103

L

Lampson, Sir Miles 19
League of Nations 83
Lebanon 72, 79
Lesser Tunb 48
Lie, Trygve 84
linkages 4–5; formation of the field of 5–8; between the Gulf and Palestine 15–25
London Conference of 1939 23–4

M

Madrid Peace Conference 95–6
Maghreb 11
majlis (legislative council) 17
majlis movement 12
majlis al-shura (consultative council) 67–8
McCloy, John 2
McFarlane, Robert 76
Mecca crisis 78
Meir, Golda 58–9, 107
Memoranda of Understanding on Strategic Cooperation 74
merchant families' committee 17
migration 4, 6, 16; *see also* refugees
militarisation, Arab 1–2
Mossadegh, Muhammad 27
Mubarak, Hosni 94
Muhammad bin Fahd, Prince of Saudi Arabia 67
Mujahideen (Afghanistan) 69, 73
Muscat and Oman 43–4

N

Nasser, Gamal Abdel 1, 2, 9, 13, 27–8, 30, 35, 37, 39, 44, 57
Nasser, Kamal 47, 105
Netherlands, The 62
networks 4–5; *see also* linkages
Nicaragua 69, 75, 76
Nixon, Richard 9, 51, 52, 54, 55, 57, 59, 106
Nixon Plan 2
Noland Amendment (1984) 75
North, Oliver 76
Nowfal, Camille 34
nuclear test ban 51

O

Occupied Territories 36
Office of Intelligence Research (OIR) 32–3
oil 5, 6, 50, 52–3, 81; embargoes 6, 26, 36–7, 44, 57–63, 81–2; fluctuations in production 70; illicit shipments 25; threat to production in 1973 55–7
Organisation of Arab Petroleum-Exporting Countries (OAPEC) 37
Organisation of the Islamic Conference (OIC) 92
Organisation of Petroleum-Exporting Countries (OPEC) 37, 61, 62–3
Ormsby-Gore, Lord 22–3
Oslo Agreements 97–8

P

Page, Howard 32
Pahlavi, Reza (Shah of Iran) 49, 65
Palestine Authority 2
Palestine Liberation Organisation (PLO) 2, 6, 15, 50–1, 63–4, 70, 72, 79, 82, 85, 86, 87, 92–4, 95–6, 97
Palestine question/problem 6, 82, 83–6
Palestinian National Authority 2
Parsons, Anthony 51

116 Index

partition 6, 22–3, 24
Peace Process 2
Peel Commission 18, 21; Report 6, 18, 21–2
personal links 15–18
Pharaon, Rashad 38
Popular Front for the Liberation of Palestine (PFLP) 95, 97
Powell, Colin 2

Q

Qasr el-Zuhur radio station 16, 18
al-Qatami, Jasim 39
Qatar 48; reactions to 1967 war 44; reactions to Suez War 31–2
Quandt, William 55

R

Rabin, Itzhak 97
radio 5–6, 16, 20–1
Ras al-Khaimah 45–6
Rashid bin Said, Shaikh 45, 48
Reagan, Ronald 14, 69, 73, 74, 77
Reagan Peace Plan 72, 79
refugees 1, 84, 93–4
Regan, P.M. 2
remittances 63
Rendel, George 19, 20
Road Map 2–3
Rockefeller, John D. 9–10
Rogers, William 51, 52, 106
Rogers Plan 2, 52–3, 106
Roosevelt, Franklin D. 3–4, 8, 23, 24–5
Rumsfeld, Donald 77
run on banks 41

S

Al Sabah, Sabah al-Ahmad 40, 42, 55
Sabra camp 79
Sadat, Anwar 50, 52, 53, 65, 72
Saddam Hussein 66, 76, 80, 93, 94, 109
Said, Sultan 44
al-Salim, Abdallah 17, 25, 39
al-Sallah, Abdallah 35
Saqqaf, Omar 38, 51, 55
Saqr bin Sultan, Shaikh 108
al-Saqr, Hamad 17
Saud, King of Saudi Arabia 8, 27–8, 29, 32, 33–4, 34–5
Saudi Air Defence Enhancement Package 73
Saudi Arabia 12, 67–8; Grand Mosque seizure 66–7; Mecca crisis 78; reactions to Suez War 32–5; relations with US after Suez 32–4; successor to UK in the Gulf states 48–9; twin pillar of US policy 8–10, 49, 68–9; US arms sales to 72–5
Saudi–Egyptian treaty (1955) 28
Sawt al-Arab 57
Sawt al-Sahil 45
Schlesinger, James 59
Schultz, George 80
Schultz peace initiative 2
Schwarzkopf, Norman 98
Scowcroft, Brent 59
Scranton, William 38
self-determination 84, 86
Shakhbut bin Sultan, Shaikh 48
Shamir, Yitzhak 95
Sharjah 18, 45
Shatt el-Arab waterway 49
Shia riots 67
Shukairy, Ahmad 83
Sick, Gary 3
Sisco, Joseph 37–8, 54, 55, 60
SoCal 29; see also ARAMCO
Stoltzfus, Bill 51
Suez Canal Zone 41, 42
Suez War 30–3
Sultan bin Saqr, Shaikh 18
al-Suwaidi, Naji 18

T

Terzi, Labib 70
Thant, U 38
Toumayan, Alec 55
Trucial Oman Scouts 45
Trucial States 44–6, 48
Truman, Harry S. 25
Turkish–Iraqi treaty (1955) 28

U

Union of Soviet Socialist Republics (USSR) 30, 58, 59, 95
United Arab Emirates (UAE) 48
United Kingdom/Britain 5, 11, 52; and Abdel Aziz 18–24; Buraimi crisis 28–9; oil embargo of 1973 59–60, 62; withdrawal from bases east of Suez 47–8
United Nations (UN) 81–90, 91, 96; emergency sessions of General Assembly 88; General Assembly 84, 88; Resolution 242 9, 38; resolutions concerning Palestine

88–90; Security Council 53, 86–8
United Nations Relief and Works Agency (UNRWA) 84–5
United States of America (USA) 3, 5, 13–14; Arab–Israeli War of 1973 51–2, 53–5; arms sales to Saudi Arabia 72–5; Desert Fox 6–7; dual containment 8, 98, 99; Iran hostage crisis 68; Irangate 75–6; Iraq–Iran War 76–7; Middle East policy in the 1990s 95, 96, 98–9; oil embargo of 1973 57–9; shift in importance of Palestine policy from UK to 24–5; twin pillar policy 8–10, 49; vetoes in UN Security Council 86, 87
al-Utaybi, Juhayman bin Sayf 66–7

V
Venice Declaration (1982) 2, 15, 70–1

Voice of the Arabs 30, 45

W
Wagner, Robert F. 24, 25
Walsh, John Patrick 51–2
Watergate 57
al-Wazir, Khalil 79
wealth 12–13, 63
Welfare Association 13
White Paper of 1939 15, 21, 24
Woodhead Commission (1938) 22, 23

Y
Yamani, Ahmad Zaki 52
Yemen 35, 37
Young, Andrew 69–70

Z
al-Zaim, Husni 103
Zayid bin Sultan, Shaikh 44–5, 48, 56–7, 60–1, 66, 103